MAMMALS

of the

Southwestern United States

and

Northwestern Mexico

Selected examples and related species

E. Lendell Cockrum
and
Yar Petryszyn

Drawings by
Sandy Truett and Helen A. Wilson

Published by
Treasure Chest Publications, Inc.
P.O. Box 5250
Tucson AZ 85703-0250

Design and Typesetting by
Casa Cold Type, Inc.

Cover Design by
Kathleen A. Koopman

Cover Illustration by
Deboragh McDonnell

Printed in the U.S.A.

Printing 10 9 8 7 6 5 4 3 2 1

ISBN 0-918080-66-5

Information Symbols

One or more of the following symbols is given with each of the major species listed in this manual.

Time of Activity

 Diurnal: active during the daytime.

 Nocturnal: active at night.

 Crepuscular: generally active at dawn or at dusk.

Status of Populations

 Eliminated in this area.

 Rare or endangered in part or all of this area.

 A game animal or fur-bearer subject to state regulations as to seasons and limits.

For current information concerning rare and endangered species and hunting and trapping laws and seasons contact your local federal or state officials as listed in your telephone directory or contact:

United States Fish and Wildlife Service,
Southwestern Region
P.O. Box 1306
Albuquerque, NM 87103

Arizona Game and Fish Department
2222 Greenway Road
Phoenix, AZ 85023

Colorado Department of Natural Resources
6060 N. Broadway
Denver, CO 80216

New Mexico Department of Game and Fish
State Capitol Complex, Villagra Bldg.
Santa Fe, NM 87503

Texas Parks and Wildlife Department
4200 Smith School Road
Austin, TX 78744

Utah State Department of Natural Resources
1636 West North Temple
Salt Lake City, UT 84116-3156

Contents

ORDER CARNIVORA—Carnivores

A Word from the Authors

This guide is designed to help interested novices add to their knowledge of native mammals. It was not designed as a technical or semitechnical reference. Persons desiring more information should consult one or more of the books listed in the Suggested Readings at the end of this guide.

This book will be most useful in southern Utah and Colorado, Arizona, New Mexico, and western Texas—all in the United States and in Sonora and Chihuahua, Mexico.

At least 198 different species of native terrestrial mammals have occurred in these states within historic times. However, only about 86 are usually recognized as being obviously distinct. These we have here listed as "major types." For example, most novices have little difficulty distinguishing between a Round-tailed ground squirrel and a Golden-mantled ground squirrel or between a California leaf-nosed bat and a Brazilian free-tailed bat, even though they have never seen or heard of these mammals. Such species are obviously different.

In contrast, even professional mammalogists often have difficultly in quickly distinguishing among a Cliff chipmunk, a Colorado chipmunk, and a Gray-collared chipmunk. Because all chipmunks are very similar in size, shape, and color, only close attention to minor differences reveals that they are different species.

In this book, each major type is illustrated, and, for each, the common and scientific names, some major identifying features, measurements, habitats, and highlights of life habits are given. The common names and scientific names used here conform with the 1987 Checklist of Vertebrates of the United States, the U. S. Territories, and Canada, a publication of the United States Fish and Wildlife Service (see Banks et al., 1987, in the Suggested Readings). Related species are only briefly mentioned at the end of the book.

The mammals are grouped into major biological categories (bats, rodents, hoofed mammals, etc.) and are listed in the sequence normally assumed by biologists as indicating relationships.

Measurements are given in both English and metric units. Values are representative, not definitive. As in all animals, including man, individual variations make a single value almost meaningless. For instance, the small size of a young animal, the large size of an old, obese individual, or the sexual dimorphism that occurs in such species as the Wapiti (adult males are much larger than adult females) all contribute to variability. However, if the values given here are interpreted as being plus or minus ten percent, then most variation of adults will be included. Measurements have been compiled from a number of sources including specimens in the mammal collection at the University of Arizona. Especially useful were the books by Hall listed in the Suggested Readings.

A distribution map shows the general region in which a mammal occurs or has occurred in the past. Notes on habitat indicate special situations within this range where the species is usually found.

Some native mammals have not done well in their interaction with human use of the land. A few have been exterminated, at least locally. Others have prospered, becoming even more numerous with human modifications of the area.

Several non-native mammals, both domestic and wild, have been introduced. Some are now the dominant mammals of various microhabitats. A partial list of domestic mammals that have been introduced to the region includes cows, horses, burros, goats, sheep, house cats, and dogs. Some have become so well established that they are now essentially "native." The Virginia opossum, the Black rat, the Norway rat, and the House mouse are examples. Others have become established only locally. These include the Fox squirrel and the Eastern gray squirrels that live in various city parks, the burros that thrive on various rangelands, the Eastern cottontail, the European rabbit, and the Nutria.

Many other exotic species have been released, either accidentally or purposefully. A few of these are surviving locally, often in a semidomestic state. The well-advertised wild animal "farms" are obvious examples.

Much of this material was originally published by Cockrum as part of the *Mammals of the Southwest*, a publication of the University of Arizona Press. Several people aided in the preparation of this manuscript. Special thanks are due Joe C. Truett for his permission to use Sandy's drawings and to Helen A. Wilson for producing additional drawings. We also thank Carolyn Cox for converting sketches of species distribution into publishable maps.

E. Lendell Cockrum and
Yar Petryszyn
1991

The Mammals

Virginia opossum

Didelphis virginiana

Order Marsupialia   **Family Didelphidae**

Identifying Features

The Virginia opossum is about the size of a house cat. Its long, hairless tail is prehensile (like that of many monkeys), the snout is long, and the ears are naked and black. The face is white; the body is covered with long, shaggy, coarse, gray hair.

Measurements

Total length, 30 inches (760 mm); tail, 12 inches (300 mm); hind foot, 2 inches (50 mm); ear, 1 inch (25 mm); weight, 10 pounds (4.5 kg).

Habitat

Opossums occur in Sonora, easternmost New Mexico, and western Texas. They have been introduced into southern Arizona and much of central New Mexico where some populations are established, especially in mountain foothills along streams.

Life Habits

Generally feeding at night, the opossum is active throughout the year. Females give birth to poorly developed young that make their way to the marsupial pouch where further development occurs. They eat almost anything available: roots, stems, fruits, melons, carrion, insects, eggs, frogs, birds, and other foods. Opossums are slow and deliberate in their movements, thus they are often run over on highways. *See related species 1.*

Virginia opossum

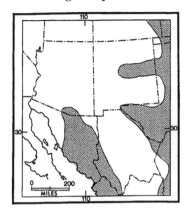

Montane shrew

Sorex monticolus

Order Insectivora   **Family Soricidae**

Identifying Features

This tiny mammal has a long snout and short, dense, velvet-like blackish to brownish fur. The belly is tinged with brown or red. The tail is the same color above and below. The eyes and ears are so reduced that they are difficult to see. The numerous teeth have reddish enamel.

Measurements

Total length, 4 inches (100 mm); tail, 1.6 inches (40 mm); hind foot, 0.5 inch (12 mm); weight, 0.20 ounce (5 g).

Habitat

These shrews live in pine forests where they are common along moist streamsides, especially in dense humus and plant cover.

Life Habits

Shrews are active at night and during the day. They usually eat about 75% of their body weight in food each day. Insects make up most of their diet, but earthworms and even small mice are also eaten. Shrews spend their lives in a small area, probably smaller than a small city lot (4000 square feet, 370 square meters). One litter is born each summer after a gestation period of about 20 days. Two to nine (usually four to six) young are born in a litter. *See related species 2-7.*

Montane shrew

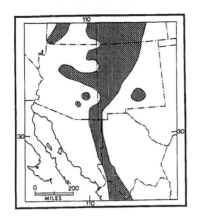

Peter's ghost-faced bat

Mormoops megalophylla

Order Chiroptera   **Family Mormoopidae**

Identifying Features

This bat has a complex area of folded skin on the lower lip. The nose is plain and the ears are short and broad. The tail is only about half the length of the interfemoral membrane (the flight membrane between the legs). The tip of the tail is free of the membrane and on its dorsal surface. Color is either a dark reddish brown or a light cinnamon brown.

Measurements

Total length, 3.7 inches (95 mm); tail, 1 inch (25 mm); hind foot, 0.5 inch (12 mm); ear, 0.6 inch (15 mm); forearm length, 2 inches (53 mm); weight, 0.5 ounce (14 g).

Habitat

Ghost-faced bats are essentially a tropical species that occur as far north as southernmost Arizona. Day roosts are in warm, moist caves or tunnels.

Life Habits

These are colonial bats, with a single roost sometimes containing 4000 to 5000 individuals. Food consists of a variety of flying insects. A single young is born in June. *See related species 8-10.*

Bats listed as numbers 11-16 are tropical forms that occur only in a very limited part of this region. They are not closely related to Peter's ghost-faced bats.

Peter's ghost-faced bat

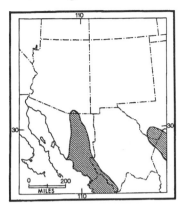

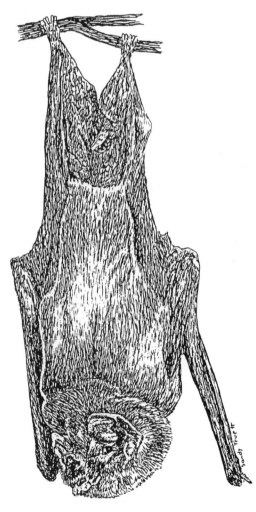

California leaf-nosed bat

Macrotus californicus

Order Chiroptera   **Family Phyllostomidae**

Identifying Features
This bat has a well-developed wedge-shaped noseleaf (flap of flesh growing up from the tip of the nose), large ears that extend forward of the tip of the nose, and are joined at their bases. The long interfemoral membrane is naked and encloses the tail.

Measurements
Total length, 3.8 inches (95 mm); tail, 1.3 inches (32 mm); hind foot, 0.6 inch (15 mm); ear, 1.3 inches (33 mm); forearm, 2 inches (50 mm); weight, 0.4 ounce (12 g).

Habitat
These bats occur in the desert below 4000 feet (1200 m).

Life Habits
These bats are active throughout the year. They are colonial, with groups of up to several hundred spending the day in warm caves or mine tunnels. On warm nights, they leave to feed on night-flying insects. On cold nights, they remain in their roost. This is a tropical species that never evolved the ability to hibernate. Mating occurs in the fall and, after a long, slow period of development, a single young is born the following June. The young grows rapidly, reaching adult size in about six weeks. *See related species 17.*

California leaf-nosed bat

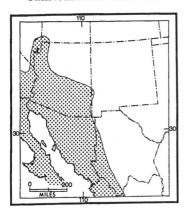

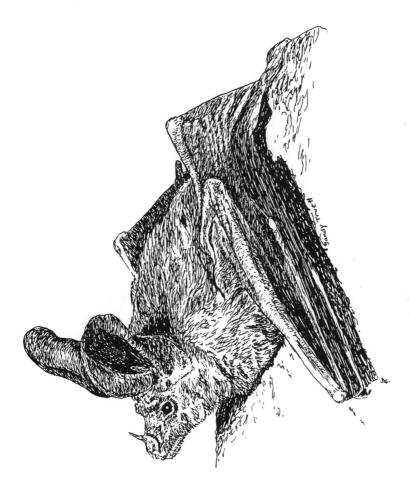

Long-tongued bat

Choeronycteris mexicana

Order Chiroptera   **Family Phyllostomidae**

Identifying Features

Long-tongued bats have a nose leaf. The head is modified for a diet of nectar: the rostrum (snout) is elongated, the ears are reduced, and the tongue is long and extensible. The extremely short tail extends only about half the length of the short interfemoral membrane.

Measurements

Total length, 3.5 inches (90 mm); tail, 1.6 inches (40 mm); hind foot, 0.5 inch (12 mm); ear, 0.7 inch (17 mm); weight, 0.6 ounce (18 g).

Habitat

During the day, Long-tongued bats roost, often singly, but sometimes in small groups, in the twilight zone of caves or mine tunnels.

Life Habits

These bats feed on the nectar and pollen of various agaves and cacti. In season, some ripe fruit is also eaten. During the late spring and early summer, females move northward (to the mountains of southern Arizona) or to higher elevations in Mexico. Usually a single young is born. Males apparently spend all summer in the more southern part of the range. *See related species 18.*

Long-tongued bat

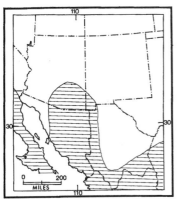

Long-nosed bat

Leptonycteris curasoae

Order Chiroptera   **Family Phyllostomidae**

Identifying Features

These bats are similar to the Long-tongued bats in shape and habits. The characteristic leaf nose is present, the snout is elongated, and the ears are reduced. The differences are that the tail is absent and the interfemoral membrane is reduced to a narrow, fur-covered ridge.

Measurements

Total length, 3 inches (75 mm); tail, absent; hind foot, 0.6 inch (15 mm); ear, 0.6 inch (16 mm); forearm, 2.1 inches (53 mm); weight, 0.6 ounce (19 g).

Habitat

Day roosts are in caves and mine tunnels in the lower desert of the southern part of the area, generally at elevations below 5000 feet (1500 m).

Life Habits

These bats feed on the nectar and pollen of various agaves and columnar cacti. In season, they feed on ripe fruits of saguaro, organ-pipe, and cardon cacti. Females start arriving at summer roosts in northern Sonora and southern Arizona in mid-April. A single young is born, usually by mid-May. When the young are able to fly, adults and young often move to higher elevations to feed on the nectar of agaves. By mid-October, they have migrated southward. Winters are spent in Mexico from southern Sonora southward. *See related species 19.*

Long-nosed bat

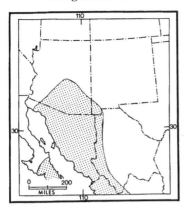

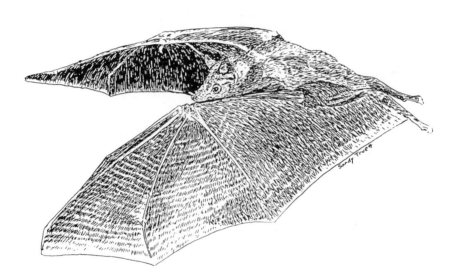

California myotis

Myotis californicus

Order Chiroptera   **Family Vespertilionidae**

Identifying Features
This plain-nosed bat has no outgrowths on its nose or lips. Its long tail is entirely surrounded by the interfemoral membrane. The ears are short, never extending more than 0.3 inch (7 mm) beyond the nose when folded forward. The tragus (fleshy outgrowth at the base of the ear opening) ends in a sharp rather than a blunt point.

Measurements
Total length, 3.2 inches (80 mm); tail, 1.5 inches (36 mm); hind foot, 0.3 inch (6.5 mm); ear, 0.5 inch (12 mm); forearm, 1.3 inches (32 mm); weight, 0.2 ounce (5 g). Weights vary to 40%, depending on time of year (heaviest in fall before hibernation or in early summer in gravid females).

Habitat
California myotis occur in deserts, grasslands, and pine forests, usually near rocky cliffs.

Life Habits
During the summer, California myotis feed on night-flying insects, storing fat that enables them to hibernate during the cold months. Day roosts are usually in rock crevices, often in groups of two to four. At night, they often hang for brief periods in abandoned buildings and mine tunnels. Winter roosts (hibernal) are in cold (not freezing) rock crevices. A single young is born each year, usually in June. *See related species 20-29.*

California myotis

Silver-haired bat

Lasionycteris noctivagans

Order Chiroptera   **Family Vespertilionidae**

Identifying Features
This plain-nosed bat has a long tail enclosed in an interfemoral membrane, the basal half of which is covered with fur. Among bats, the color is unique—being black—with the tips of many hairs being white. The result is a silvery appearance.

Measurements
Total length, 4 inches (102 mm); tail, 1.7 inches (43 mm); hind foot, 0.4 inch (10 mm); ear, 0.6 inch (16 mm); forearm, 1.6 inches (41 mm); weight, 0.4 ounce (10 g).

Habitat
Silver-haired bats are most common in montane forests at elevations above 4000 feet (1200 m).

Life Habits
These bats feed on small night-flying insects, mainly moths. Feeding generally begins after dark. Usually day roosts are single bats in trees, often under bits of bark or in shallow holes. One or two young are born in late June or early July. During cold months, some of these bats migrate down mountains where, on warm nights, they feed. On cold nights, however, they remain inactive and hibernate. Others make a north-south seasonal migration, spending the summer as far north as southern Canada and the winter in the southern United States.

Silver-haired bat

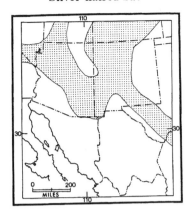

Western pipistrelle

Pipistrellus hesperus

Order Chiroptera   **Family Vespertilionidae**

Identifying Features

This is the smallest bat in the United States. The tail and inter-femoral membrane are relatively long. Each ear has a short, rounded tragus (fleshy vertical growth on lower edge of ear). The color is light, usually buff gray, with a black mask across the eyes.

Measurements

Total length, 2.8 inches (72 mm); tail, 1.3 inches (32 mm); hind foot, 0.2 inch (5 mm); ear, 0.5 inch (13 mm); forearm, 1.2 inches (30 mm); weight, 0.1 ounce (3 g).

Habitat

This species occurs most commonly in cliff areas. Rock-walled canyons, usually at elevations below 5000 feet (1500 m), are favored homes.

Life Habits

Pipistrelles are generally solitary, roosting in rock crevices in canyon walls. Small groups have been found roosting in crevices in brick buildings and behind window shutters. The evening flight starts early, often before sundown. At dusk, these bats feed on small insects captured in flight. The young are born in late June or early July. Two young per litter are usual. Males generally spend the winter months at lower elevations and actively feed during warm evenings, while females generally move to higher, colder elevations and hibernate. *See related species 30.*

Western pipistrelle

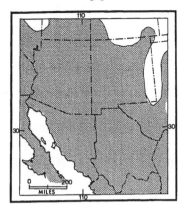

Big brown bat

Eptesicus fuscus

Order Chiroptera   **Family Vespertilionidae**

Identifying Features

This plain-nosed bat has a long tail in a naked interfemoral membrane and short ears. It is sometimes confused with the Little brown myotis, from which it differs in larger size and having a blunt tragus. The wing and interfemoral membranes are almost black.

Measurements

Total length, 4 inches (102 mm); tail, 1.5 inches (39 mm); hind foot, 0.4 inch (11 mm); ear, 0.6 inch (16 mm); forearm, 1.9 inches (47 mm); weight, 0.6 ounce (16 g).

Habitat

Big brown bats occurs at a wide range of elevations, from sea level to timberline. They live in forests as well as in more open areas.

Life Habits

In the summer, Big brown bats may have day roosts in buildings, hollow trees, and other similar situations. Winters are spent in hibernation in cold rock crevices and caves at higher elevations. Food consists of night-flying insects. Females give birth to one or two young, usually in mid-June. During the fall, bats that spent the summer at low elevations migrate to cooler, higher elevations and hibernate.

Big brown bat

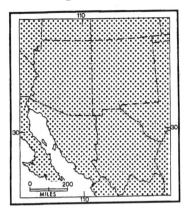

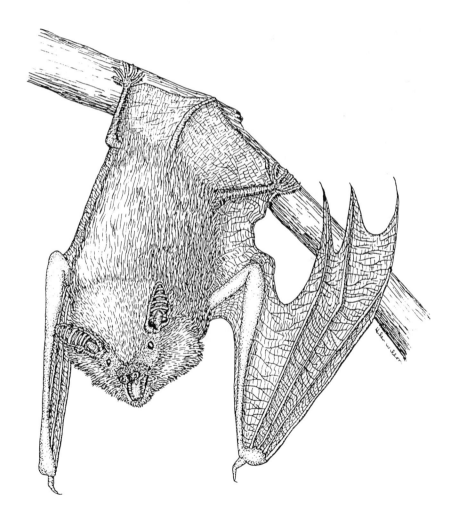

Red bat

Lasiurus blossevillii

Order Chiroptera   **Family Vespertilionidae**

Identifying Features

This plain-nosed bat has a long tail enclosed in a fur-covered interfemoral membrane. Its ears are small. The pelage color is bright orange-red to buff, with scattered white-tipped hairs.

Measurements

Total length, 4.3 inches (108 mm); tail, 1.7 inches (43 mm); hind foot, 0.3 inch (7 mm); ear, 0.4 inch (10 mm); forearm, 1.7 inches (42 mm); weight, 0.4 ounce (12 g).

Habitat

Red bats roost in trees, either in forests at high or low elevations or in the scattered trees along streams or washes in the desert or desert grasslands. Those that spend the summer at high elevations migrated down slope or southward to spend the winter.

Life Habits

Red bats feed after dark. They capture flying insects, especially those that occur along the edges of tree clumps or over water surrounded by trees. Day roosts are in clumps of leaves in trees. Roosting is solitary except that a female hangs in a cluster with her young. Two to four young are born in late June or early July.

Red bat

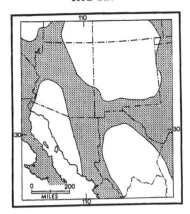

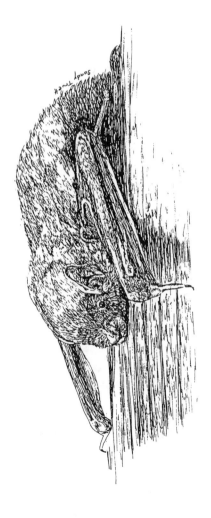

Hoary bat

Lasiurus cinereus

Order Chiroptera   **Family Vespertilionidae**

Identifying Features

This bat is similar to the Red bat but is much larger. The back is yellowish to dark brown. It has a frosted (hoary) appearance because many hairs are white-tipped. The interfemoral membrane and the lower surface of the arms and legs are covered with fur.

Measurements

Total length, 5.6 inches (142 mm); tail, 1.9 inches (49 mm); hind foot, 0.5 inch (13 mm); ear, 0.7 inch (17 mm); forearm, 2.1 inches (53 mm); weight, 1 ounce (28 g).

Habitat

Hoary bats are rarely found beyond forests.

Life Habits

Hoary bats feed entirely on night-flying insects. They spend the day roosting singly among the leaves of a tree. Females usually give birth to two young, generally in late June or early July. Seasonal migrations occur, either from northern areas southward or from high southern mountains down slope to low elevations. Hoary bats are strong fliers and probably can make long flights during a single night.

Hoary bat

Southern yellow bat

Lasiurus xanthinus

Order Chiroptera   **Family Vespertilionidae**

Identifying Features

This species is similar to the Red bat in size, but differs in color (yellowish to buff with only a few white-tipped hairs), and has only the basal half of the interfemoral membrane covered with hair.

Measurements

Total length, 4.4 inches (110 mm); tail, 2 inches (50 mm); hind foot, 0.4 inch (9 mm); ear, 0.6 inch (16 mm); weight, 0.5 ounce (13 g).

Habitat

Southern yellow bats are associated with palm trees. Most of the range of this species is in Mexico and Central America.

Life Habits

These bats are apparently residents throughout the year although they are rarely seen in the winter. Day roosts are usually among the dead fronds of palm trees. They feed on night-flying insects after total darkness. Like other tree-roosting species, they hang alone in day roosts. A litter of two young is born in early June.

Southern yellow bat

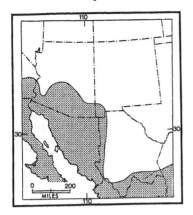

Spotted bat

Euderma maculatum

Order Chiroptera   **Family Vespertilionidae**

Identifying Features

This plain-nosed bat has unique, extremely large, pink-colored ears and black fur that has three dorsal white spots, one on each shoulder and one on the rump. The long tail is enclosed in a naked interfemoral membrane.

Measurements

Total length, 4.3 inches (110 mm); tail, 1.9 inches (48 mm); hind foot, 0.4 inch (11 mm); ear, 1.8 inches (44 mm); forearm, 1.9 inches (49 mm); weight, 0.6 ounce (17 g).

Habitat

Spotted bats are rarely seen and little understood by biologists. They have been taken from hot, low deserts as well as at elevations up to 8000 feet (2400 m). Day roosts are probably in deep rock crevices in high canyon walls.

Life Habits

Spotted bats have been observed only during the warm seasons. Like the related Townsend's big-eared bats, they probably hibernate during the cold season and make only a short local trip to the winter roost. Food consists of night-flying insects. This unusual bat is known from a few locations in the western United States and from one location in Chihuahua, Mexico.

Spotted bat

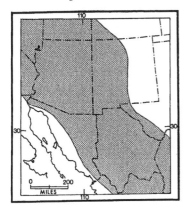

Townsend's big-eared bat

Plecotus townsendii

Order Chiroptera   **Family Vespertilionidae**

Identifying Features

This large-eared, plain-nosed bat has a long tail encased in a long, naked interfemoral membrane. It has large ears joined at their inner bases. A pair of prominent glandular lumps occur on each side of the snout.

Measurements

Total length, 3.9 inches (100 mm); tail, 1.8 inches (45 mm); hind foot, 0.4 inch (9 mm); ear, 1.4 inches (35 mm); forearm, 1.6 inches (40 mm); weight, 0.4 ounce (9 g).

Habitat

Townsend's big-eared bats occur in wooded and forested regions. Day roosts are generally in caves but are sometimes in the attics of buildings.

Life Habits

These bats feed entirely on night-flying insects. They are very agile in flight and can hover and pick insects from plant leaves. During the summer, small numbers (up to 50) congregate in a maternity colony. A single young is born in mid-June. Most winter roosts are in rock crevices at higher elevations. These bats can't tolerate much human disturbance and many populations are now reduced or extinct in areas of high human density. *See related species 31-32.*

Townsend's big-eared bat

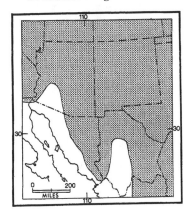

Pallid bat

Antrozous pallidus

Order Chiroptera   **Family Vespertilionidae**

Identifying Features

This plain-nosed, big-eared bat has a long tail encased in a long interfemoral membrane. The body structure is stout. The color is light, with individual hairs creamy white, tipped with brown or black.

Measurements

Total length, 4.7 inches (120 mm); tail, 1.8 inches (46 mm); hind foot, 0.4 inch (10 mm); ear, 1.2 inches (30 mm); forearm, 2.2 inches (55 mm); weight, 0.7 ounce (20 g).

Habitat

Pallid bats are most common in the lower elevations but, at least in the summer, occur from high mountains to low deserts.

Life Habits

These bats feed on a variety of large arthropods, including sphinx moths, scarab beetles, grasshoppers, crickets, and scorpions. The prey is carried to a night roost (often a shallow cave, mine tunnel, or house porch) where the soft parts are eaten and the hard wings and legs are dropped. The results are piles of bat droppings and insect parts. During the summer, day roosts are in the attics of buildings, crevices in bridges, or similar places. Winter habits are poorly known but they probably hibernate in crevices at higher elevations in nearby rocky areas. Two (sometimes one) young are born in June.

Pallid bat

Brazilian free-tailed bat

Tadarida brasiliensis

Order Chiroptera   **Family Molossidae**

Identifying Features

Free-tailed bats have a significant portion of the tail extending posterior to the interfemoral membrane. The flight membranes are dark, thick, and leathery in appearance. The ears are flattened, thickened, and extend forward over the eyes. The hind feet have well-developed tactile hairs.

Measurements

Total length, 4 inches (100 mm); tail, 1.3 inches (34 mm); hind foot, 0.4 inch (10 mm); ear, 0.7 inch (17 mm); forearm, 1.7 inches (42 mm); weight, 0.4 ounce (12 g).

Habitat

Brazilian free-tailed bats are most common at lower elevations but, at least in the summer, occur from high mountains to low deserts.

Life Habits

These colonial bats sometimes congregate in colonies of millions, such as the famous group at Carlsbad Caverns, New Mexico. However, most resident summer roosts in this area do not contain more than a few hundred individuals. These feed on night-flying insects, especially small moths. The single young is born in late June. Most migrate southward during the fall. *See related species 33-35.*

Brazilian free-tailed bat

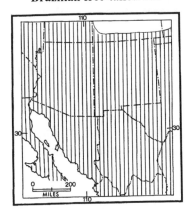

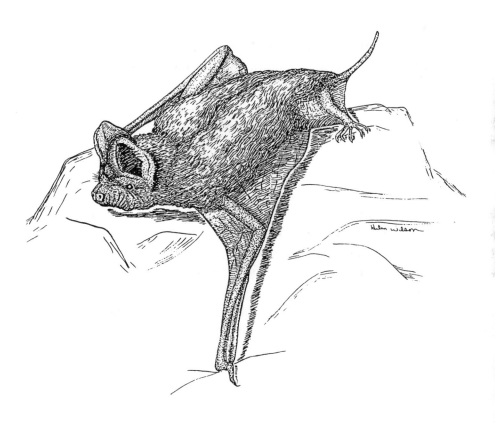

Western mastiff-bat

Eumops perotis

Order Chiroptera   **Family Molossidae**

Identifying Features

Like the Brazilian free-tailed bat, this bat has part of the tail extending beyond the interfemoral membrane. It has thick flight membranes and tactile hairs on the feet. The Western mastiff-bat differs in being much larger and in having the low, flattened ears fused at the inner base. This is the largest bat in the area, having a wingspan of about 21 inches (530 mm).

Measurements

Total length, 7.2 inches (185 mm); tail, 2.2 inches (55 mm); hind foot, 0.7 inch (17 mm); ear, 1.6 inches (41 mm); weight, 2.1 ounces (60 g).

Habitat

Western mastiff-bats are usually found in desert areas with high rocky cliffs that are near large bodies of permanent water.

Life Habits

These large bats feed entirely on night-flying insects. Day roosts are small colonies (up to 50 individuals) hanging in rock crevices high above a canyon floor. A few roosts have been found in the attics of two-story buildings. Because these bats have such narrow wings, they cannot take off in flight from a flat surface. They must first climb up some surface, then drop, set their wings, and become airborne. The single young is born in late June or early July. *See related species 36.*

Western mastiff-bat

Pika

Ochotona princeps

Order Lagomorpha   **Family Ochotonidae**

Identifying Features

About the size of a guinea pig, the Pika is a small, short-eared, short-legged, rabbitlike mammal that has a short tail hidden by fur. The upper parts are grayish to buff in color. The underparts are lighter and are washed with buff.

Measurements

Total length, 8 inches (200 mm); tail, 0.6 inch (16 mm); hind foot, 1.2 inches (30 mm); ear, 1 inch (25 mm); weight, 4.4 ounces (125 g).

Habitat

North American Pikas live in higher mountains in close association with rock slides. In this region, they occur in the higher elevations of northern New Mexico.

Life Habits

Pikas are active during the day. They define territories by characteristic calls (whistles) and scent marks. Food consists of various green plants that are eaten or harvested, spread on rocks to dry, and stored for use in the winter season. This stored "hay" is well-hidden in dry places that are readily reached during the winter months when green plants are dead or covered by ice and snow. Two to five (generally three) naked, blind young are born in a fur-lined nest in May or June. They reach adult size by mid-summer.

Pika

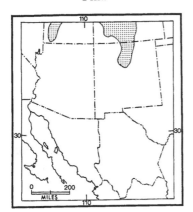

Eastern cottontail

Sylvilagus floridanus

Order Lagomorpha   **Family Leporidae**

Identifying Features

This medium-sized cottontail has relatively short ears and a characteristic rusty-colored patch at the nape of the neck. The inner surface of the ears have only scattered hairs.

Measurements

Total length, 16.5 inches (420 mm); tail, 2.2 inches (55 mm); hind foot, 3.5 inches (90 mm); ear, 2.4 inches (62 mm); weight, 3.3 pounds (1.5 kg).

Habitat

In the western part of their range, these cottontails are common in grassy areas of the oak woodlands, especially along streams and washes.

Life Habits

Cottontails eat various grasses, herbs, and other green vegetation. They are most active in the early morning and late evening, but become almost completely nocturnal during the summer. After a gestation of about four weeks, the young are born in the warmer months. Three or four litters, each consisting of four to seven young, are born in an underground fur-lined nest. At birth, the young are hairless, blind, and helpless. Maturity is reached nine to ten months after birth. *See related species 37-38.*

Eastern cottontail

Black-tailed jack rabbit

Lepus californicus

Order Lagomorpha   **Family Leporidae**

Identifying Features

This hare has both large hind legs and big ears. Its upper parts are grayish, the belly and most of the tail are white. The top of the tail and the tips of the ears are black.

Measurements

Total length, 22.6 inches (575 mm); tail, 3.2 inches (80 mm); hind foot, 5.7 inches (145 mm); ear, 4.3 inches (110 mm); weight, 4.5 pounds (2.1 kg).

Habitat

Black-tailed jack rabbits live at low elevations, from sea level up to about 5000 feet.

Life Habits

During the summer, these jack rabbits feed on a variety of green plants. During the winter, they feed on the buds and bark of shrubs. They are generally active at night, but are seasonally crepuscular (active in late afternoon and early morning). One to seven young (usually four) are born in a litter and more than one litter per year is normal. The young are precocial (born fully haired and with open eyes), and are able to follow their mother within a few minutes after their birth. *See related species 39-40.*

Black-tailed jack rabbit

Antelope jack rabbit

Lepus alleni

Order Lagomorpha   **Family Leporidae**

Identifying Features

This is a large version of the Black-tailed jack rabbit and is the largest rabbit in the Western Hemisphere. Its ears are without a black terminal spot. Color is a light gray with top and sides of head washed with buff.

Measurements

Total length, 30 inches (626 mm); tail, 2.6 inches (65 mm); hind foot, 5.3 inches (135 mm); ear, 7.1 inches (180 mm); weight, 9 pounds (4.1 kg).

Habitat

Antelope jack rabbits occur in Sonora on the west side of the Sierra Madre Mountains, northward into the upper parts of the Sonoran Desert in south-central Arizona.

Life Habits

Habits of the Antelope jack rabbit are similar to those of the Black-tailed jack rabbit. Daylight hours are usually spent resting in the shade of a cactus or low desert bush. In the dry season, they often feed on various cacti. The number of young per litter is one to five with two being common. Three or four litters per year are usual. These large jack rabbits escape most predators by simply outrunning them. As they run away, they often turn to the side, pulling up the white belly fur as a "flash," and then turn abruptly away. *See related species 41.*

Antelope jack rabbit

Yellow-bellied marmot

Marmota flaviventris

Order Rodentia   **Family Sciuridae**

Identifying Features

This large, heavyset, ground squirrel-shaped animal has small ears and a short tail. Its color is varied, usually tan or brownish, and often washed with white. An obvious white patch is present between the eyes.

Measurements

Total length, 23.6 inches (600 mm); tail, 8 inches (200 mm); hind foot, 3.2 inches (80 mm); ear, 1 inch (25 mm); weight, to 20 pounds (9 kg). Variations are about 15%, in part because growth continues after adult status is reached.

Habitat

Marmots are usually found in rocky places, often along road cuts in mountainous situations.

Life Habits

Marmots eat plants, especially grasses. They are active during the warm months. In northern mountains, they may be active for only three months of the year. Much fat is stored in the short summer. During the long hibernation, half of the body weight is lost. Adult size is reached in the third year, even though some females have young in their second year. A dominant male defends a territory of about 1.5 acres (0.6 hectares) from other males. Several females and young may live in this territory. A litter of four or five young is common.

Yellow-bellied marmot

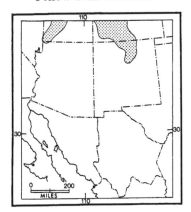

Least chipmunk

Tamias minimus

Order Rodentia   **Family Sciuridae**

Identifying Features
Chipmunks have five evenly spaced longitudinal stripes on the back, three short lateral stripes on each side of the head, and a long, well-haired tail. The belly is usually buff, bright orange, or a grayish yellow. The ears are relatively long and pointed.

Measurements
Total length, 7.7 inches (195 mm); tail, 3.5 inches (90 mm); hind foot, 1.2 inches (30 mm); ear, 0.6 inch (16 mm); weight, 1.8 ounces (50 g).

Habitat
These chipmunks generally live at higher elevations, often some distance from pine trees.

Life Habits
Food consists of many kinds of seeds, berries, fruits, fungi, and other plant material. In some areas, juniper berries, acorns, and pine nuts are eaten. Some insects are also eaten. Four to six young per litter is common and some females have two litters in a year. They store various seeds in underground burrows. Most of the cold season is spent in hibernation. *See related species 42-47.*

Least chipmunk

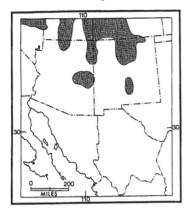

Harris' antelope squirrel

Ammospermophilus harrisii

Order Rodentia   **Family Sciuridae**

Identifying Features

Antelope squirrels differ from other small squirrel-like rodents in that they have a well-developed white stripe extending on each side from the shoulder to the hip and have no central dark stripes. The bushy tail is usually held curved over the back, exposing a buff-colored lower surface.

Measurements

Total length, 9.1 inches (230 mm); tail, 3 inches (75 mm); hind foot, 1.5 inches (38 mm); ear, 0.5 inch (12 mm); weight, 4.4 ounces (125 g).

Habitat

Restricted to the low deserts of Arizona and northwestern Sonora.

Life Habits

These diurnal ground squirrels are active most of the year. On very cold winter days, they remain below ground. On hot summer days, they are most active in the early morning. Food consists of seeds, berries, fruits, insects, and green vegetation. Buds and new growth of mesquite and various cactus fruits are seasonal favorites. Each individual uses several short, shallow burrow systems for protection from heat and enemies as well as places to store seeds. During February or March, a litter of five to nine young is born in an underground nest chamber lined with soft vegetation and hair. *See related species 48-49.*

Harris' antelope squirrel

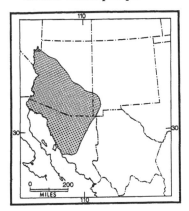

Thirteen-lined ground squirrel

Spermophilus tridecemlineatus

Order Rodentia   **Family Sciuridae**

Identifying Features

This small ground squirrel has a characteristic pattern of alternating dark and light stripes. A row of squarish white spots is in the center of each of the dark stripes. The dark stripes vary from brown to blackish. The tail is bushy.

Measurements

Total length, 9.3 inches (235 mm); tail, 3 inches (75 mm); hind foot, 1.3 inches (33 mm); ear, 0.4 inch (10 mm); weight, 4.6 ounces (130 g).

Habitat

These ground squirrels are generally found in well-drained sites in short-grass grasslands.

Life Habits

Unlike many other ground squirrels, these are solitary, living in underground burrows that rarely show any sign of a mound at the entrance. Food consists of seeds, green plants, and many insects. Hibernation may last five to six months. Mating occurs in the spring and, after a gestation period of 28 days, a litter of five to 13 young is born in an underground nest. *See related species 50-51.*

Thirteen-lined ground squirrel

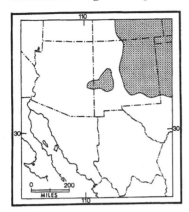

Rock squirrel

Spermophilus variegatus

Order Rodentia   **Family Sciuridae**

Identifying Features

These large ground squirrels, with long, bushy tails and mottled gray backs, are sometimes confused with tree squirrels. They differ in that the ears are quite short. The tail is longer than that of the tree squirrels, not as bushy, has no distinct white fringe, and often has alternating rings of dark and light colored hairs.

Measurements

Total length, 19 inches (475 mm); tail, 8 inches (200 mm); hind foot, 2.4 inches (60 mm); ear, 1.2 inches (30 mm); weight, 1.7 pounds (760 kg).

Habitat

Rock squirrels occur in rocky places in a wide range of habitats from high mountains to the desert edge.

Life Habits

These semicolonial animals are inactive between November and February, even in warm places. Activity in the summer is from dawn to dusk. They eat flowers, fruits, seeds, and green growth. Locally they are pests, feeding on various crops, even nuts and fruits. A litter of five to eight young is common. Young are usually born during the summer, but some litters appear aboveground as early as late June and others as late as mid-September.

Rock squirrel

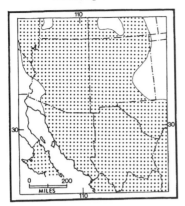

Round-tailed ground squirrel

Spermophilus tereticaudus

Order Rodentia   **Family Sciuridae**

Identifying Features

This small ground squirrel is light colored above, generally some shade of cinnamon. The belly is a lighter shade. The tail is not bushy but is covered with short hairs.

Measurements

Total length, 9.5 inches (240 mm); tail, 2.8 inches (70 mm); hind foot, 1.4 inches (35 mm); ear, 0.2 inch (6 mm); weight, 5 ounces (140 g).

Habitat

Round-tailed ground squirrels live in sandy soils at lower elevations in the Sonoran Desert.

Life Habits

These animals spend the coldest parts of winter in hibernation. However, during warm periods in midwinter, they may be active aboveground. They are active during the day. In hot weather, most feeding is done in the early morning. During mid-day, they go into their cool underground burrow to escape the heat. They feed on almost any green vegetation but will eat seeds, flowers, and cactus fruit. One large litter (4-12, usually 5 or 6) born in April is usual, but some females may have a second litter in July.

Round-tailed ground squirrel

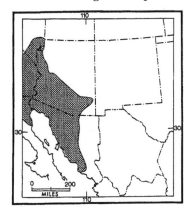

Golden-mantled ground squirrel

Spermophilus lateralis

Order Rodentia   **Family Sciuridae**

Identifying Features

These mountain-inhabiting ground squirrels with lateral stripes are commonly confused with chipmunks. They differ in that there is no stripe on the side of the head. They have a white stripe running from the shoulder to the hips on each side of the dark back. The short, bushy tail, edged with white, is gray to yellowish below.

Measurements

Total length, 10.8 inches (275 mm); tail, 3.7 inches (95 mm); hind foot, 1.7 inches (42 mm); ear, 0.8 inch (20 mm); weight, 7 ounces (200 g).

Habitat

This species generally occurs in meadows or glades of evergreen forests in higher mountains.

Life Habits

These mammals feed during the daytime on buds, young leaves, flowers, seeds, berries, nuts, and fungi. Insects are also readily taken. Food is stored in the burrow. A litter of four to eight young is born in late spring. By early fall, both adults and young are fat and enter hibernation. At higher elevations, this winter sleep may last six months. *See related species 52.*

Golden-mantled ground squirrel

Gunnison's prairie dog

Cynomys gunnisonii

Order Rodentia   **Family Sciuridae**

Identifying Features

The prairie dog is a large rodent that is chunky bodied. Its short, white-tipped tail has a mid-dorsal gray streak. The coat color is a uniform cinnamon buff, above and below.

Measurements

Total length, 13.8 inches (350 mm); tail, 2.4 inches (60 mm); hind foot, 2.2 inches (55 mm); ear, 0.5 inch (12 mm); weight, 2 pounds (900 kg).

Habitat

Prairie dogs occur in areas of compact, well-drained soil in open grasslands. Often the ground is slightly sloping.

Life Habits

Prairie dogs live in colonies of up to 200 or more. Some large colonies are measured in the thousands and cover areas measured in square miles. The colonies have a complex social system with various divisions (termed wards). They communicate by calls, by body position (such as tail up, tail down), and by odors. Such things as a hawk flying nearby (danger to all), and stranger in the neighborhood being identified and told to leave are all communicated. Food consists of various plant materials (especially short grasses), roots, bulbs, worms, and insects. *See related species 53.*

Gunnison's prairie dog

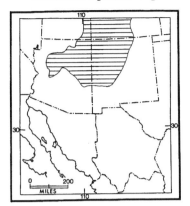

Sandy Truett

Abert's squirrel

Sciurus aberti

Order Rodentia   **Family Sciuridae**

Identifying Features

This large tree squirrel has a tuft of hair on the tip of the ears and a dark-colored back. The underparts are white. The tail is long and bushy.

Measurements

Total length, 22 inches (550 mm); tail, 10.2 inches (260 mm); hind foot, 2.8 inches (70 mm); ear, 1.5 inches (38 mm); weight, 1.5 pounds (680 kg).

Habitat

Abert's squirrels occur in ponderosa pine forests.

Life Habits

Tree squirrels are active throughout the year. Most of their activity is in the early morning and late afternoon. During cold stormy periods, they remain in the nest for days at a time. Food includes a range of plant materials including leaf buds, flowers, herbs, fungi, berries, and especially the seeds and buds of ponderosa pines. A litter of three or four young is born in May or June. Sometimes a second litter is born as late as September. Populations on the North Rim of the Grand Canyon are considered by some to be a separate species—the Kaibab squirrel (*Sciurus kaibabensis*).

Abert's squirrel

Nayarit squirrel

Sciurus nayaritensis

Order Rodentia   **Family Sciuridae**

Identifying Features

This large tree squirrel is closely related to the Fox squirrel of the eastern United States. Its dorsal color is yellowish brown, the underparts are more yellowish. The long, bushy tail has buff-tipped hairs.

Measurements

Total length, 22 inches (570 mm); tail, 10.5 inches (270 mm); hind foot, 2.8 inches (70 mm); ear, 1.3 inches (35 mm); weight, 1.8 pounds (800 kg).

Habitat

This species occurs in the oak-pine zone of the Sierra Madre Mountains and adjacent mountains.

Life Habits

These squirrels feed on a variety of fruits, fungi, seeds, buds, and other plant material, as well as nuts. Activity is generally in the daytime, with most occurring in the mornings, especially in the warmer times of the year. During the coldest months, much time is spent sleeping in a nest of twigs and leaves high in a tree. The population in the Chiricahua Mountains of Arizona has been variously recognized as a separate species—sometimes as Chiricahua squirrel (*Sciurus chiricahuae*) and also Apache squirrel (*Sciurus apache*). *See related species 54.*

Nayarit squirrel

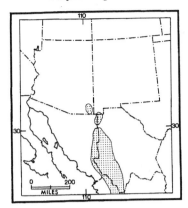

Sandy Truett

Arizona gray squirrel

Sciurus arizonensis

Order Rodentia   **Family Sciuridae**

Identifying Features
This tree squirrel is similar to Abert's squirrel but has no ear tufts. It is distinguished from the Nayarit squirrel by its white belly and from the Rock squirrel by its tail being clearly edged in white and the back uniform in color.

Measurements
Total length, 21 inches (535 mm); tail, 9.8 inches (250 mm); hind foot, 2.8 inches (70 mm); ear, 1.2 inches (30 mm); weight, 1.4 pounds (650 kg).

Habitat
The Arizona gray squirrel is usually seen in canyons and the rim country in areas where oaks, walnuts, and some pine are present.

Life Habits
Gray squirrels are active throughout the year, usually in the early morning and late afternoon. During cold stormy periods, they remain in their nest for days at a time. Food is a variety of plant materials including leaf buds, flowers, herbs, fungi, and berries. Much food, especially various nuts, is gathered and stored in hollow trees or in shallow holes in the ground. One litter (sometimes two) of three or four young is born each summer, between May and September. *See related species 55.*

Arizona gray squirrel

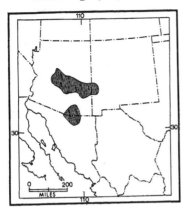

Red squirrel

Tamiasciurus hudsonicus

Order Rodentia   **Family Sciuridae**

Identifying Features

This is the smallest of the tree squirrels. It has prominent black stripes, one on each side. Its tail is narrow and shorter than the head and body. Black-tipped hairs occur along the edge and the end of the tail. The dorsal coat color is dark reddish to yellowish; the belly is yellowish. This squirrel is usually heard calling before it is seen.

Measurements

Total length, 12.8 inches (325 mm); tail, 4.9 inches (125 mm); hind foot, 1.9 inches (50 mm); ear, 1 inch (25 mm); weight, 8.1 ounces (230 g).

Habitat

Red squirrels generally live in spruce forests high in the mountains, usually above 7000 feet (2100 m) in elevation.

Life Habits

These squirrels are active throughout the year. In cold stormy weather, they remain in their nests. They feed during the day. In summers, most activity is during mornings. Food includes fungi, nuts, and seeds. They often carry food to a "feeding stump" where they watch surroundings as they extract the food from nuts or cones. After some time, a huge stack of debris accumulates at the site. Nests are in hollow trees or are built of twigs and bark high in the tree. Two litters of two to seven young are born, one in April or May and another as late as September.

Red squirrel

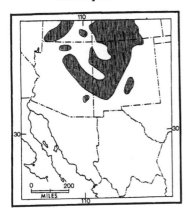

Sandy Truett

Southern flying squirrel

Glaucomys volans

Order Rodentia   **Family Sciuridae**

Identifying Features

The combination of prominent fur-covered gliding membranes along the sides between the fore and hind legs, and soft silky fur is unique to flying squirrels. The ears are small and the bushy tail is broad and flattened. Dorsal color is brownish, the tail is blackish, and the belly is white to creamy white.

Measurements

Total length, 10 inches (250 mm); tail, 4 inches (100 mm); hind foot, 1.1 inches (29 mm); ear, 1 inch (25 mm).

Habitat

Flying squirrels are forest dwellers, being most common in dense coniferous areas. In this region, flying squirrels are known only from one locality in the Sierra Madre Mountains.

Life Habits

Flying squirrels are the only North American members of the squirrel family that are not active during the day. As a result, they are rarely seen and little known by most people. They are active throughout the year. Their food consists of seeds, nuts, fungi, berries, insects, and even small birds. Nests are constructed of shredded bark in hollow trees. Sometimes they will build a roof over an abandoned bird nest and use it as a retreat. After a gestation period of 40 days, a litter of two to five young is born in May or June.

Southern flying squirrel

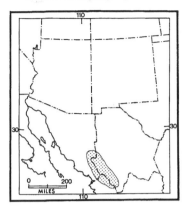

Botta's pocket gopher

Thomomys bottae

Order Rodentia   **Family Geomyidae**

Identifying Features

Rarely seen aboveground, this medium-sized rodent has many modifications for life in an underground burrow: the forefeet have elongated claws for digging, the ears are tiny, the wide head is flattened and wedge-shaped, the neck is short, the body is stout. Color is light in dry areas and almost black in moist regions.

Measurements

Total length, 9.5 inches (240 mm); tail, 3 inches (75 mm); hind foot, 1.3 inches (32 mm); ear, 0.4 inch (10 mm); weight, 6.7 ounces (190 g). Variation is plus or minus 25%. Pocket gophers that live in deep soils are usually larger.

Habitat

Pocket gophers occur mainly in soft soil. They are common in grasslands and meadows; alfalfa fields are favored sites.

Life Habits

Gophers feed on vegetation, mostly in long feeding tunnels underground. Roots and bulbs are most commonly taken, but whole plants may be pulled into a burrow and eaten. A nest is built in a deep tunnel, often under a rock or the roots of a bush or tree. Generally there is only one gopher in a tunnel system that may have 20 or more earth mounds on the surface. Two to ten young per litter and one or two litters each year is normal. *See related species 56-60.*

Botta's pocket gopher

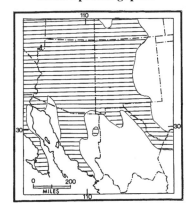

Silky pocket mouse

Perognathus flavus

Order Rodentia   **Family Heteromyidae**

Identifying Features

This small mouse has soft fur, a wide head, short neck, and tiny ears. Its tail is not tufted and is longer than the head and body. Color is generally light pinkish buff above and white below. Well-developed fur-lined cheek pouches occur on each side of the head.

Measurements

Total length, 4 inches (100 mm); tail, 1.8 inches (45 mm); hind foot, 0.6 inch (16 mm); ear, 0.2 inch (6 mm); weight, 0.3 ounce (8 g).

Habitat

The Silky pocket mouse is common in deserts and sandy areas in desert grasslands.

Life Habits

These pocket mice spend the cold season in hibernation. They become active aboveground in late spring and disappear under-ground in early fall. They construct burrows, usually with three or four openings, under bushes. These mice are active at night. They feed on the seeds of many grasses and other small plants. Some insects and some green plants are eaten, especially in the spring. Usually seeds are collected and transported in the fur-lined cheek pouches to storage places in the burrows. A litter of three to six young is born after a four-week gestation period. Two litters each summer are common. *See related species 61-65.*

Silky pocket mouse

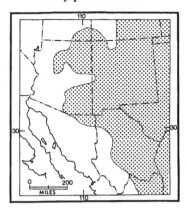

Rock pocket mouse

Chaetodipus intermedius

Order Rodentia   **Family Heteromyidae**

Identifying Features

This is a larger version of the previous species. Its hair is harsh and its color is darker, usually a grayish buff above. The belly is whitish. It has distinct brown and light-colored spines on the rump. The tail is longer than the head and body and has a weakly developed tuft of hairs at the tip. Fur-lined cheek pouches are present.

Measurements

Total length, 6.7 inches (170 mm); tail, 4 inches (100 mm); hind foot, 0.9 inch (20 mm); ear, 0.3 inch (7 mm); weight, 0.5 ounce (15 g).

Habitat

Rock pocket mice are common inhabitants of rocky areas. Most of the relatives of this species occur in desert situations.

Life Habits

Like other pocket mice, this species is strictly nocturnal. Active from early spring to early fall, they spend the cold months in hibernation. Their burrow is generally constructed under a bush or next to a rock. Food consists mostly of seeds but green vegetation and insects are also eaten. Seeds are collected and stored in the burrow system. One or two litters of two to seven young are born each year. *See related species 66-73.*

Rock pocket mouse

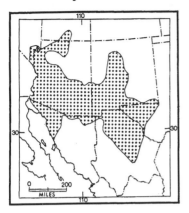

Merriam's kangaroo rat

Dipodomys merriami

Order Rodentia   **Family Heteromyidae**

Identifying Features

Kangaroo rats are modified for jumping (saltatorial) locomotion. The hind legs and feet are enlarged, the forelimbs are small. The tail is long and has a well-developed tuft of hair at the tip. A white stripe runs across the thighs. The color of the back is generally tan, buff, or cinnamon. The belly has long, soft, white hairs.

Measurements

Total length, 9.8 inches (250 mm); tail, 5.9 inches (150 mm); hind foot, 1.5 inches (40 mm); ear, 0.5 inch (14 mm); weight, 1.6 ounces (44 g).

Habitat

These kangaroo rats live in a variety of situations, from grasslands to low deserts, where open areas make their jumping locomotion useful.

Life Habits

These nocturnal, seed-eating rodents store food in shallow holes in the ground or in their burrows. Various insects and newly sprouted seeds are also eaten. Kangaroo rats are active throughout the year. One to six, usually three, young are born in a litter. In the warmer parts of its range, this species has two litters in a year, one in the winter and one in the summer. *See related species 74-78.*

Merriam's kangaroo rat

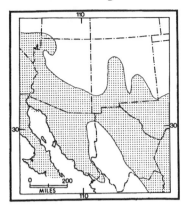

Beaver

Castor canadensis

Order Rodentia   **Family Castoridae**

Identifying Features

The large size and the adaptations for a life in and around water make the Beaver quite distinct. It has webbed hind feet; a large, flattened, scale-covered tail; and small ears. The pelage is long, dense, and water repellant.

Measurements

Total length, 36 inches (980 mm); tail, 16 inches (400 mm); hind foot, 6.7 inches (170 mm); ear, 1.3 inches (33 mm); weight, 50 pounds (23 kg).

Habitat

Beaver live in or along permanent streams and lakes that are bordered by trees. In the desert, they occur along the Colorado River. They are now reduced in numbers and are exterminated in some areas.

Life Habits

These rodents generally live in family groups. Slapping the tail on water and other devices are used for communication. Beavers feed on the bark and outer layers of various bushes and trees, especially aspens, birches, and willows. They may build a dam of sticks, rocks, and mud across small streams, making a "beaver pond." They may also construct a dome-shaped lodge of sticks and mud that has an underwater entrance. In some places, "lodges" are constructed as burrows in stream banks. A litter (two to eight kits) is born in April or May.

Beaver

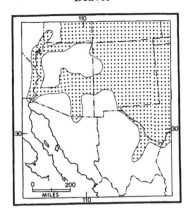

Western harvest mouse

Reithrodontomys megalotis

Order Rodentia   **Family Muridae**

Identifying Features

This small mouse has small ears; a long, slender, sparsely haired tail; and no external fur-lined cheek pouches. A vertical groove is present on the front of each upper incisor. It is brownish above, white below, and the sides have a line of buff-colored fur between the dorsal and ventral colors.

Measurements

Total length, 5.5 inches (140 mm); tail, 2.6 inches (65 mm); hind foot, 0.7 inch (17 mm); ear, 0.5 inch (12 mm); weight, 0.4 ounce (12 g).

Habitat

Harvest mice occur in grassy areas. They are most numerous in grasslands and mountain meadows.

Life Habits

These mice feed on seeds and plant growth. Most activity is at night but they may feed during the day. Harvest mice are active throughout the year. They rest in a nest of grass at ground level or sometimes in a low bush. The nest is sometimes a modification of a bird's nest. The breeding season is April to October. After 23 days, a litter of one to seven helpless, hairless, and blind young is born. Two or more litters may be produced each summer. *See related species 79-81.*

Western harvest mouse

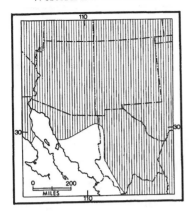

Deer mouse

Peromyscus maniculatus

Order Rodentia   **Family Muridae**

Identifying Features

Deer mice are similar to Harvest mice but are larger, especially in the length of the ears and the diameter of the tail. There is no groove on the front surface of the upper incisor. Colors vary from dark grayish to a light buff brown above and are white below. The tail is white with a narrow, distinct dark stripe on the dorsal surface. Young, like the young of most members of this family, are a light gray in their first coats of fur.

Measurements

Total length, 7.1 inches (180 mm); tail, 3.1 inches (80 mm); hind foot, 0.9 inch (22 mm); ear, 0.7 inch (17 mm); weight, 1 ounce (28 g).

Habitat

These mice are most common in grasslands, but some live in small grassy areas surrounded by dense forests. Related species occur in almost all habitats in the area.

Life Habits

Deer mice are active at night throughout the year. They construct short underground burrows with a nest of grasses or other soft material. Woodland dwellers may construct their nest in a hollow log. Their diet includes insects and other arthropods, but is mainly fungi, berries, fruits, small nuts, and seeds. After a gestation of 28 days, a litter of three to seven young is born. *See related species 82-91.*

Deer mouse

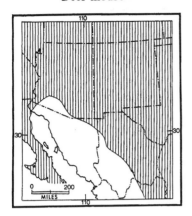

Northern pygmy mouse

Baiomys taylori

Order Rodentia   **Family Muridae**

Identifying Features

This tiny mouse is smaller than the Western harvest mouse and has a very short, hair-covered tail. Unlike Harvest mice, there is no groove on the front surface of the upper incisors. The pelage is dark brownish-gray, soft, and shaggy. The ears are smaller and more rounded than those in the Deer mouse.

Measurements

Total length, 4.1 inches (105 mm); tail, 1.8 inches (45 mm); hind foot, 0.6 inch (14 mm); ear, 0.4 inch (11 mm); weight, 0.4 ounce (10 g).

Habitat

In this region, Pygmy mice are restricted to grasslands along the desert edge.

Life Habits

Pygmy mice are active throughout the year. They construct small runways through the grass that can often be detected by the tips of cut grass strewn along the trail. They feed mainly on grass shoots and some other green plant material. Litter size is small, ranging from one to three with two being most common.

Northern pygmy mouse

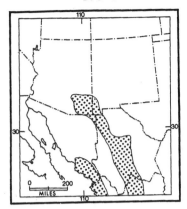

Southern grasshopper mouse

Onychomys torridus

Order Rodentia   **Family Muridae**

Identifying Features

This plump-bodied mouse has a short, thick tail and relatively short legs. The tail, less than half the length of the head and body, is thick and constricted at the base. The back is generally pale cinnamon to light brown. The belly and feet are white.

Measurements

Total length, 5.3 inches (138 mm); tail, 1.6 inches (40 mm); hind foot, 0.8 inch (20 mm); ear, 0.7 inch (17 mm); weight, 1.2 ounce (35 g).

Habitat

Grasshopper mice are dwellers of sandy, vegetated areas in the desert and desert grasslands.

Life Habits

This species, active at night throughout the year, is more of a carnivore than other small rodents. Food consists mainly of invertebrates, especially grasshoppers. They hunt in small groups and have a high-pitched whistle that apparently helps keep the group together. Each group has a system of burrows: a central nest burrow (closed during the day), food storage burrows (seeds for use when insects are not available), and a series of short escape burrows throughout the normal hunting territory. A litter of four to five naked, blind young is born after a gestation period of 30 to 45 days. Two litters per year are common. *See related species 92-93.*

Southern grasshopper mouse

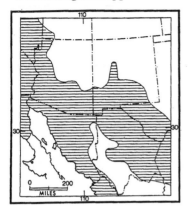

Hispid cotton rat

Sigmodon hispidus

Order Rodentia   **Family Muridae**

Identifying Features

This species is the size of a small rat. The coat is coarsely grizzled, generally blackish or brownish mixed with buff or gray. The sides and belly are lighter than the back. The tail is shorter than the head and body.

Measurements

Total length, 9.8 inches (250 mm); tail, 4.1 inches (105 mm); hind foot, 1.3 inches (32 mm); ear, 0.7 inch (17 mm); weight, 3.2 ounces (90 g).

Habitat

In this area, the Hispid cotton rat occurs in tall grasses and weed-grown fields.

Life Habits

This species, active throughout the year, often feeds during the day. They have cleared runways along which are often found small stacks of short pieces of grass stems. Food is mainly the stems and new growth of grasses and weeds. Their nest, constructed of grasses, is under piles of dead vegetation or even in abandoned Pocket gopher burrows. After a gestation period of four weeks, a litter of two to ten blind, naked young is born. One female may have as many as nine litters in one year. Some may be born during almost every month, but most are born between June and October. *See related species 94-97.*

Hispid cotton rat

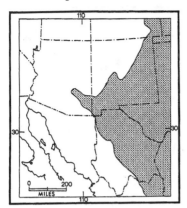

White-throated woodrat

Neotoma albigula

Order Rodentia   **Family Muridae**

Identifying Features
This large rat has a tail that is thick, round, blunt-ended, covered with short hairs and is shorter than the head and body. The
ears are large and naked. The fur is soft, dense, and, like the
tail, is dark above and white below. Woodrats usually build a
characteristic pile of sticks and other material around nest sites.

Measurements
Total length, 15 inches (375 mm); tail, 6 inches (150 mm); hind
foot, 1.5 inches (37 mm); ear, 1.4 inches (35 mm); weight, 6.3
ounces (180 g).

Habitat
Often called Pack rats, White-throated woodrats live in a wide
range of habitats at the forest edge, often near rock ledges, and
in bushy areas down into the low desert. Most are found in areas
of dense stands of cacti, especially cholla and prickly pears.

Life Habits
These nocturnal rats are active throughout the year. Food includes a wide variety of plant materials, including stems and
leaf shoots of trees and, especially, parts of various cacti. The
den may be only a grass-lined nest under a few sticks in a rock
crevice or a large heap of sticks and other debris, often under-
neath a large cactus. Two litters (March and May) are common,
each with two to four young. *See related species 98-103.*

White-throated woodrat

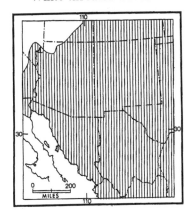

Bushy-tailed woodrat

Neotoma cinerea

Order Rodentia   **Family Muridae**

Identifying Features
This woodrat is large, thickly furred, and has a bushy squirrel-like tail that is shorter than the head and body. Its ears are large and are bare on the tips. The coat is soft, dark above and white on the belly.

Measurements
Total length, 15.8 inches (400 mm); tail, 5.1 inches (130 mm); hind foot, 1.7 inches (52 mm); ear, 1.4 inches (35 mm); weight, 10.6 ounces (300 g).

Habitat
This species occurs at the forest edge, often near rock ledges, and sometimes in caves, mines, and abandoned buildings.

Life Habits
Habits are much like those of the White-throated woodrat. Food includes fungi and a wide variety of herbs, including stems and leaf shoots of trees. Some insects are also eaten. They build a den that may vary from a simple grass-lined nest under a few sticks in a rock crevice to a large heap of sticks and other debris, often in an abandoned building. Two litters (March and May) are common, each with two to four young. They are often called trade rats because they often drop whatever they happen to be carrying back to the den and pick up some bright object such as a spoon or ring.

Bushy-tailed woodrat

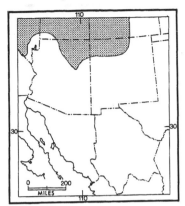

Southern red-backed vole

Clethrionomys gapperi

Order Rodentia   **Family Muridae**

Identifying Features

This small, chunky mouse has a short tail and short ears. Its coat consists of long, grizzled hairs. A broad dorsal stripe ranges in color from bright chestnut to yellowish brown.

Measurements

Total length, 6 inches (150 mm); tail, 2 inches (50 mm); hind foot, 0.7 inch (20 mm); ear, 0.5 inch (13 mm); weight, 1 ounce (28 g).

Habitat

These voles are most common in forested mountains above 8000 feet (2500 m). They usually live near or under decaying logs.

Life Habits

These mice are active throughout the year. Their activities are not restricted to the night. During winter, they construct feeding tunnels under the snow. Food is almost entirely vegetation. A fungus (*Endogone*) that grows on decaying leaves and wood makes up all of the food of some individuals. Sprouting seeds are also eaten. Three to eight (usually four) young are born in a litter and more than one litter per summer is common. The nest is usually only a small pile of soft vegetation under a log or in a burrow under a root.

Southern red-backed vole

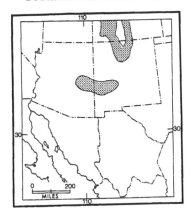

sandy Truett

Heather vole

Phenacomys intermedius

Order Rodentia   **Family Muridae**

Identifying Features

This is a chunky, short-snouted mouse with short ears; large, bead-like eyes; and long, loose, soft grizzled pelage. It looks much like the preceding species but lacks the rusty or reddish stripe down the back and its short tail is sharply bicolored, dark above and white below. The feet are white.

Measurements

Total length, 5.5 inches (140 mm); tail, 1.4 inches (35 mm); hind foot, 0.8 inch (18 mm); ear, 0.6 inch (15 mm); weight, 1.3 ounces (37 g).

Habitat

Heather voles are not common anywhere. They live in grassy and heather patches near water, in high mountains.

Life Habits

Voles are active in early evening and at night throughout the year. In the winter, they construct nests of soft grasses and lichens aboveground under snow. At other times, the nest is underground. Food includes lichens, green plants, berries, and tree bark. After 21 days, a litter of two to eight blind, naked, and helpless young is born. One female may have three litters in a year.

Heather vole

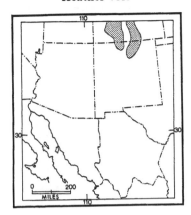

Long-tailed vole

Microtus longicaudus

Order Rodentia   **Family Muridae**

Identifying Features

At first glance, this looks like either of the two preceding species. It is a chunky, short-snouted mouse with short ears; large bead-like eyes; and long, loose, grizzled hair. It differs in being darker colored, brownish gray above, and having dark feet. Its habitat (dense grass) and habit of constructing narrow runways through dense grass that often are sunk into the ground are usually enough to distinguish this species.

Measurements

Total length, 7.2 inches (184 mm); tail, 2.4 inches (62 mm); hind foot, 0.8 inch (21 mm); ear, 0.5 inch (10 mm); weight, 1.6 ounces (50 g).

Habitat

These voles live in grasslands and open grassy meadows, from 4300 to over 11,000 feet. They live in well-developed runways among the roots of grasses or in ground litter.

Life Habits

Long-tailed voles are active throughout the year. Food is green vegetation. Roots, stems, and leaves are all eaten. A nest of grass is built aboveground. In a single year, a female may give birth to as many as ten litters, each with two to eight blind, naked young. *See related species 104-107.*

Long-tailed vole

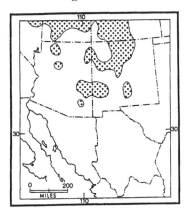

Muskrat

Ondatra zibethicus

Order Rodentia   **Family Muridae**

Identifying Features
This large rodent is adapted for living in and near water. The tail is scaly, laterally compressed, and about the length of the head and body. The toes of the hind feet are fringed with stiff hairs that aid in swimming.

Measurements
Total length, 20 inches (500 mm); tail, 10 inches (250 mm); hind foot, 2.8 inches (72 mm); ear, 0.8 inch (20 mm); weight, 4 pounds (1.8 kg).

Habitat
Muskrats live in and around permanent streams, lakes, and ponds through most of this area, even up to elevations of 11,000 feet (3400 m).

Life Habits
Muskrats, active at night throughout the year, eat any plant that grows in or near water. They also eat crops such as corn when available. Dens are constructed as domed structures of vegetation and mud that rise above the water and have an entrance below water. At times, dens are dug in the banks of streams or lakes, utilizing underwater entrances. One to 11 (usually six) young are born in a litter. At high elevations and in the north, two litters are common while at low elevations in the south, three or four litters may be produced.

Muskrat

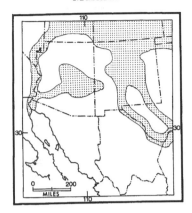

Norway rat

Rattus norvegicus

Order Rodentia   **Family Muridae**

Identifying Features

This rat resembles the Woodrat in general size, but differs in having short ears and a sparsely haired, scaly tail that is slightly shorter than the head and body. The back, belly, and feet are grayish, with some brownish tones on the back.

Measurements

Total length, 14.6 inches (370 mm); tail, 6.5 inches (170 mm); hind foot, 1.4 inches (36 mm); ear, 0.9 inch (22 mm); weight, 10 ounces (280 g).

Habitat

This rat is rarely found in undisturbed natural situations, but occurs in buildings, trash heaps, city dumps, and other places that have been modified by humans.

Life Habits

This native of the Old World lives with humans throughout most of the world. Norway rats eat a wide variety of crops and stores of animal and human foods. Its reproductive rate is high. A litter has two to 20 young, and up to nine litters are born in one year. Adulthood is reached in 90 to 120 days. These rats are carriers of a series of diseases including plague, typhus, and spotted fever. The white and hooded rats of the pet store and the laboratory are special varieties of this species. *See related species 108.*

Norway rat

House mouse

Mus musculus

Order Rodentia   **Family Muridae**

Identifying Features

This mouse is about the same size and shape as the Western harvest mouse, but its tail is long, scaly, hairless, and is gray both above and below. The belly is usually grayish but sometimes has a whitish or buff wash. The upper incisors are not grooved, but do have a distinctive notch in the grinding surface when viewed from the side.

Measurements

Total length, 6.7 inches (170 mm); tail, 3.1 inches (80 mm); hind foot, 0.7 inch (18 mm); ear, 0.5 inch (13 mm); weight, 0.7 ounce (20 g).

Habitat

This mouse is rarely found in undisturbed natural situations, but is generally in and around buildings and agricultural areas.

Life Habits

Like the Norway rat, the House mouse is a native of the Old World that has also adapted to living with man throughout most of the world. They eat a wide variety of food: crops, stored animal and human food, as well as insects. When food is available, they are capable of producing several litters (up to 14) of up to 16 young in a year. Nests are of soft material in hidden places, such as holes in the ground, in walls, or under boards.

House mouse

Western jumping mouse

Zapus princeps

Order Rodentia   **Family Dipodidae**

Identifying Features

This is a rather large mouse that has large hind feet, enlarged hind legs and an elongated tail. It is adapted for leaping (saltatorial) locomotion. The upper incisors are grooved on the front surface. The back is dark, the sides yellowish or buff, the belly white. The ears are short and edged with light hairs.

Measurements

Total length, 9.5 inches (240 mm); tail, 5.7 inches (145 mm); hind foot, 1.3 inches (32 mm); ear, 0.6 inch (16 mm); weight, 0.8 ounce (23 g).

Habitat

This species occurs mainly in mountains between 4000 and 11,000 feet (1300-3400 m), especially under aspens and willows.

Life Habits

Jumping mice are active during the night in the warmer parts of the year. They hibernate during the cold months. Food consists of insects, fungi, and a series of berries and seeds. They become very fat in the fall, some gaining almost 25% of their body weight in three weeks before entering hibernation. Nests are grass-lined structures in underground burrows. A litter of two to seven young is born early in the summer. The scientific name to be applied to populations in eastern Arizona is being debated.

Western jumping mouse

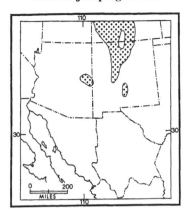

Porcupine

Erethizon dorsatum

Order Rodentia   **Family Erethizontidae**

Identifying Features
This large rodent (larger than a small dog) has specialized hair in the form of spines (quills) on the back, sides, and tail. It is chunky-bodied and has short legs. The claws (four front, five behind) are long and curved.

Measurements
Total length, 35 inches (890 mm); tail, 8.3 inches (210 mm); hind foot, 4.3 inches (110 m); ear, 1.2 inches (30 mm); weight, 18 pounds (8.2 kg).

Habitat
Porcupines are most common in evergreen forests. However, in this area, they are found almost anywhere there are trees, from sea level to above timberline.

Life Habits
Porcupines are active, generally at night, throughout the year. They feed on a variety of plants. Most noticeable is the bark that is stripped from the trunks and branches of trees, especially in the winter. Twigs, leaves, stems of various trees, and herbs are also eaten. They are usually solitary and have a den in a cave, crevice, or hollow tree. After a gestation period of about 120 days, a single young (sometimes twins) is born, usually in late spring.

Porcupine

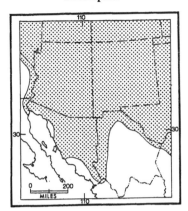

Coyote

Canis latrans

Order Carnivora   **Family Canidae**

Identifying Features

The Coyote looks very much like a small German shepherd dog. It is buff gray or grizzled above, buff below, and has a black-tipped bushy tail.

Measurements

Total length, 47 inches (1.2 m); tail, 14 inches (350 mm); hind foot, 7.9 inches (200 mm); ear, 4.3 inches (110 mm); weight, 23 pounds (10.5 kg).

Habitat

Coyotes occur from high mountains to low deserts. They are often common on rangelands and in the suburbs of towns and cities.

Life Habits

Coyotes are usually most active in early morning and late afternoon throughout the year. Some are active at night and on cooler overcast days. They have been reported as the best runners among the wild dogs. They can run for long distances at about 25 miles per hour and can dash up to 40 mph. Food consists of a wide range of animal and vegetable matter. Rodents, rabbits, and insects as well as juniper berries, cactus fruit, and berries are commonly eaten. Some deer and domestic livestock are killed by coyotes, but most eaten by them had died of other causes and was eaten as carrion. During the spring, a litter of up to 11 pups is born in an underground den.

Coyote

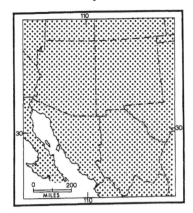

Sandy Truett

Gray wolf

Canis lupus

Order Carnivora   **Family Canidae**

Identifying Features

A small wolf is similar in size and general appearance to a large Coyote or a very large German shepherd. Even experts are sometimes uncertain of sight identifications. Coat color varies from light buff to almost black. Differences include: nose pad 1 inch (25 mm) or more wide (smaller in coyotes and dogs), tail held out behind when running (between the legs in coyotes).

Measurements

Total length, 78 inches (2 mm); tail, 18 inches (450 mm); hind foot, 12 inches (300 mm); ear, 4 inches (100 mm); weight, 110 pounds (50 kg). Males are about 20% larger than the females.

Habitat

The wolf formerly occurred in most of this area, perhaps only rarely in the low deserts. It is now probably exterminated, although sightings are still being reported in the Sierra Madre Mountains and in southeastern Arizona.

Life Habits

Generally, wolves lived in small family groups consisting of an adult female, her mate, the young of the year, and perhaps the young of her previous litter. Members of the group often joined in a wolf pack for hunting. The annual hunting range of such a group was as much as 50 miles (80 km) in length and perhaps as wide. Timber wolf and Lobo are names that were applied to local populations.

Gray wolf

Red fox

Vulpes vulpes

Order Carnivora   **Family Canidae**

Identifying Features

This dog-shaped carnivore has long, pointed ears, a long muzzle, and a very bushy, white-tipped tail. Dorsal color is usually a reddish yellow shade. The feet are black.

Measurements

Total length, 43 inches (1.1 mm); tail, 17 inches (430 mm); hind foot, 6.7 inches (170 mm); ear, 3.3 inches (85 mm); weight, 10 pounds (4.5 kg).

Habitat

Red foxes occur only in wooded areas in the northeastern part of this region.

Life Habits

These foxes are active throughout the year, mostly in the early evening and at night. Food consists of insects and small rodents. Occasionally a rabbit is taken as are some fruits and berries. They generally live in burrows or in a rock crevice. The same den is often occupied by generation after generation of foxes. A litter of one to eight pups is born in late spring or early summer. The female, male, and young live and hunt as a family unit until the young leave the next year.

Red fox

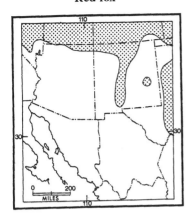

Sandy Tivett

Kit fox

Vulpes macrotis

Order Carnivora   **Family Canidae**

Identifying Features

The Kit fox looks much like a small, light-colored Red fox with unusually large ears. It is the smallest fox in the Americas. The back is a yellowish gray; the underparts white. The tail is black-tipped and the feet and ears are buff.

Measurements

Total length, 31 inches (790 mm); tail, 10 inches (250 mm); hind foot, 5 inches (125 mm); ear, 3.3 inches (85 mm); weight, 4.5 pounds (2 kg). The females are slightly smaller than the males.

Habitat

Kit foxes live in deserts and desert grasslands. Much of their distribution coincides with that of the larger kinds of kangaroo rats.

Life Habits

Kit foxes are active at night throughout the year. They have a den in an underground burrow. The den usually has three or four escape tunnels. Food includes kangaroo rats, pocket mice, some rabbits, and some insects. A litter of four or five young is born in March or April. *See related species 109.*

Kit fox

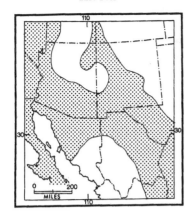

Gray fox

Urocyon cinereoargenteus

Order Carnivora   **Family Canidae**

Identifying Features

This fox is similar to the Red fox, but is darker in color, has a tail that is larger, a dorsal stripe of stiff black hairs, and is tipped with black. The color of the back ranges from grizzled grayish to reddish. The throat is white and the chest, sides, and belly are reddish.

Measurements

Total length, 37 inches (940 mm); tail, 17 inches (425 mm); hind foot, 5.3 inches (135 mm); ear, 2.6 inches (65 mm); weight, 8.4 pounds (3.8 kg). Females are smaller than males.

Habitat

Gray foxes occur in deserts, open forests, and brush from sea level to 9000 feet (2800 m).

Life Habits

Habits of the Gray foxes are similar to those of the other foxes. They are more secretive than other species. Almost all of their activity is at night. Food consists of a mixture of plant and animal materials. Juniper berries, fruits, acorns, insects, birds, and especially small mammals are included in their diet. This species can climb trees to get to food or to escape an enemy. It has a den in a hollow log, under a boulder, or in a rock crevice. A litter of two to five young is born in the spring.

Gray fox

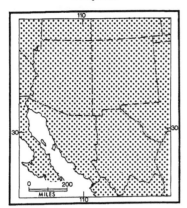

Black bear

Ursus americanus

Order Carnivora   **Family Ursidae**

Identifying Features
This large, heavily built, short-tailed carnivore is usually black in color, above and below. Some are cinnamon; others are almost tan. The feet are short and broad.

Measurements
Total length, 63 inches (1.6 m); tail, 3.5 inches (90 mm); hind foot, 9.5 inches (240 mm); ear, 5 inches (125 mm); weight, 250 pounds (120 kg). Females are smaller than the males. Sometimes old males reach weights of about 500 pounds.

Habitat
Bears are mostly restricted to forested and wooded areas, especially at intermediate elevations. Now absent in cultivated areas, they are locally more common than they were 100 years ago.

Life Habits
Bears are most active at night, but sometimes are active even in the middle of the day. During cold periods, they spend most of their time sleeping. They have a den in a hollow tree, rock crevice, or hole in the ground. Bears are omnivorous, feeding on a wide range of plant and animal material. Fruits, berries, acorns, plant shoots, roots, bulbs, fish, insects, rodents, rabbits—all are eaten. One to four cubs are born in late winter. The young are small (about 1.5 pounds [0.7 kg]), blind, and helpless at birth.

Black bear

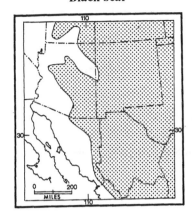

Grizzly bear

Ursus arctos

Order Carnivora   **Family Ursidae**

Identifying Features

The Grizzly bear is larger than the Black bear. It is a yellowish brown to black in dorsal color and has a prominent hump at the shoulders.

Measurements

Total length, 85 inches (2.1 m); tail, 4 inches (100 mm); hind foot, 12 inches (300 mm); ear, 5 inches (125 mm); weight, 900 pounds (400 kg).

Habitat

Grizzly bears formerly lived in mountains and along major streams in the lowlands. They are now exterminated in this area.

Life Habits

Habits of these bears are similar to those of Black bears. Food consists of almost any edible material. Dead animals are fed upon as is garbage and food in campgrounds. They have a larger feeding territory (up to 25 miles in diameter) than the Black bear. After a gestation period of about 180 days, two or three tiny, almost hairless, blind cubs are born. Adult size is reached in the third year. In captivity, they live for as long as 34 years.

Grizzly bear

Ringtail

Bassariscus astutus

Order Carnivora   **Family Procyonidae**

Identifying Features

This is a small-bodied, long-tailed carnivore that is somewhat catlike in general form. The tail has alternating bands, eight black and eight white. The tip of the tail is black. The back is a yellowish gray, the belly is whitish.

Measurements

Total length, 31 inches (790 mm); tail, 15 inches (380 mm); hind foot, 3 inches (75 mm); ear, 2 inches (50 mm); weight, 2.2 pounds (1 kg).

Habitat

Ringtails generally live in areas of rock exposures, commonly in rocky canyons below 6000 feet (1800 m) in elevation.

Life Habits

Ringtails are active throughout the year, almost entirely at night. They feed mainly on small rodents, especially wood rats and other species that also live in rocky situations. Lizards, birds, insects, and other invertebrates are also taken. In season, they do eat various fruits and berries. Their den is in a rock crevice, a shallow cave, a hollow tree, and even in abandoned buildings. After a gestation period of about 53 days, a litter of two to four blind, fuzzy young are born in May or June. Ringtails live up to eight years in captivity.

Ringtail

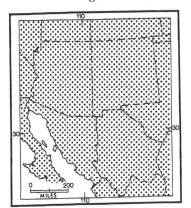

Raccoon

Procyon lotor

Order Carnivora   **Family Procyonidae**

Identifying Features

The Raccoon is a stout-bodied carnivore with a ringed, bushy tail somewhat resembling that of the Ringtail. The face has a well-developed dark mask around the eyes. The back is a mixture of dark and light-colored hairs. The black-tipped tail has five to seven black rings with rings of yellowish white hairs in between.

Measurements

Total length, 30 inches (750 mm); tail, 11 inches (280 mm); hind foot, 4.7 inches (120 mm); ear, 2.2 inches (55 mm); weight, 22 pounds (10 kg). Some old, fat males weigh as much as 40 pounds.

Habitat

Raccoons are common in areas of permanent water, along streams and irrigation canals, generally at elevations below 6000 feet (1800 m).

Life Habits

Raccoons are active throughout the year, mostly after dark. Much of their food is taken along streams. It includes fish, frogs, invertebrates, birds, mice, and a range of vegetable material. Grains, fruits, and melons are all eaten when available. One to six (usually four) blind, helpless young are born in April or May in a den hidden under a boulder, in a hollow tree, or similar place.

Raccoon

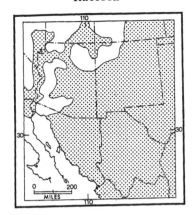

Coati

Nasua nasua

Order Carnivora   **Family Procyonidae**

Identifying Features

Coatis are somewhat like a raccoon in general appearance but have a greatly elongated nose that terminates in a flattened "rooting" pad. The hind limbs are much larger than the fore-limbs. The long tail has poorly marked rings.

Measurements

Total length, 41 inches (1050 mm); tail, 20 inches (500 mm); hind foot, 3.6 inches (91 mm); ear, 1.6 inches (40 mm); weight, 25 pounds (11 kg). Females are up to 25% smaller than the males.

Habitat

Coatis are most common in oak woodlands and in adjacent grasslands in the southern part of this region.

Life Habits

Coatis are most active during the daylight hours. They often feed in bands of up to 50 individuals. They feed by rooting in the ground for debris on the forest floor, exposing and capturing insects, small mammals, and various invertebrates. They are excellent climbers and feed on fruits, berries, bird eggs, and other foods found in trees. A litter of four to six naked, blind young is born in the spring or early summer after a gestation period of about 75 days.

Coati

Marten

Martes americana

Order Carnivora   **Family Mustelidae**

Identifying Features

The Marten is a long-bodied, short-legged carnivore with cat-like ears. It is the size of a large tree squirrel. The back is a golden brown color, the throat and chest are yellowish. The belly is slightly paler than the back. The fur is dense, soft, and in high demand for fur coats. The feet and tip of the tail are black.

Measurements

Total length, 25.5 inches (650 mm); tail, 8.3 inches (210 mm); hind foot, 3.3 inches (85 mm); ear, 1.6 inches (40 mm); weight, 2 pounds (0.9 kg). The females are as much as 25% smaller than the males.

Habitat

Martens are forest dwellers, occurring most commonly at high elevations in dense forests of fir and spruce.

Life Habits

Martens are active throughout the year, generally at night. They feed in trees as well as on the ground. Food consists of small mammals (especially Red squirrels), birds, insects, and some fruits and berries. They usually have a den in a hollow log or hollow tree, but sometimes rest in the branches of a tree. Up to five blind, helpless young are born in a litter, usually in April. In captivity, a Marten has lived as long as 17 years.

Marten

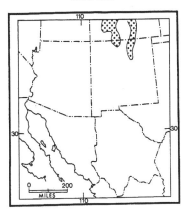

Long-tailed weasel

Mustela frenata

Order Carnivora   **Family Mustelidae**

Identifying Features

The weasel shape is well-known: small, short-legged, long-bodied. The Long-tailed weasel has a black-tipped tail that is about half the length of the head and body. The back is brownish in color, the belly is yellowish white. During winter in the northern part of this area, the color is white except for the black-tipped tail.

Measurements

Total length, 16 inches (410 mm); tail, 5 inches (125 mm); hind foot, 2 inches (50 mm); ear, 0.8 inch (20 mm); weight, 9.5 ounces (270 g). The males are larger and almost twice the weight of the females.

Habitat

Long-tailed weasels occur from low grasslands to high mountains. They are usually near water.

Life Habits

These weasels are active throughout the year, mainly at night. Most activity is on the ground and in underground burrows of other animals. They sometimes climb trees to reach food. Their den, often a nest originally built by some other mammal, is usually under a pile of rocks or under a tree stump. They feed on small rodents, and, to a lesser extent, on birds and bird eggs. A litter (usually five) of blind, helpless young is born in mid-April.

Long-tailed weasel

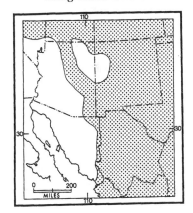

Ermine

Mustela erminea

Order Carnivora   **Family Mustelidae**

Identifying Features
This is the smallest carnivore in the area. It has the typical weasel shape (short-legged, long-bodied, short-eared). Its black-tipped tail is only about a third of the length of the head and body. The color is brown above, whitish below. Like the Long-tailed weasel, its winter color is white except for the black-tipped tail.

Measurements
Total length, 10 inches (250 mm); tail, 2.4 inches (60 mm); hind foot, 1.2 inches (30 mm); ear, 0.6 inch (14 mm); weight, 1.8 ounces (50 g). Females are smaller than the males.

Habitat
Ermines occur in a wide variety of situations, especially along bushy streams, in fence rows, and on rocky hillsides. They do not occur in the low deserts.

Life Habits
Ermines are active throughout the year, mainly at night. They feed entirely on small animals, especially mice. Lizards, birds, rats, even small rabbits are also killed and eaten. Their den is in a burrow, usually under a fallen tree, boulder, or other protected situation. A litter of four to eight blind, helpless young is born in the spring. The male helps in feeding the young by bringing food to the den.

Ermine

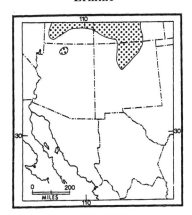

Black-footed ferret

Mustela nigripes

Order Carnivora   **Family Mustelidae**

Identifying Features

This large, pale-colored weasel has a distinct black face mask. The feet and tip of the tail are brownish-black to black. The back is a pale yellowish buff. The throat and belly are almost white.

Measurements

Total length, 19 inches (500 mm); tail, 4 inches (100 mm); hind foot, 2.4 inches (60 mm); ear, 1.2 inches (30 mm); weight, 1.5 pounds (700 g).

Habitat

Black-footed ferrets occurred in prairie dog towns. They have now been eliminated from this area.

Life Habits

Black-footed ferrets are active throughout the year, mainly at night. Their habits have never been adequately documented. According to several authors, this species may depend on prairie dog burrows for shelter and prairie dogs may make up most of their food. It is now on the Endangered Species list of the United States Fish and Wildlife Service. Any observations should be reported to a game biologist or a park naturalist.

Black-footed ferret

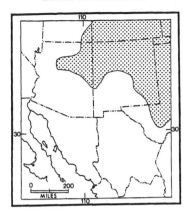

Mink

Mustela vison

Order Carnivora   **Family Mustelidae**

Identifying Features

This large weasel has dense, water-repellant fur. The color is
dark brown, darkest on the tip of the tail and on the middle of
the back. The tail is about half of the length of the head and
body. Unlike other weasels, its belly is dark. A white chin patch
is usually present.

Measurements

Total length, 24 inches (600 mm); tail, 7 inches (175 mm); hind
foot, 2.8 inches (70 mm); ear, 0.6 inch (15 mm); weight, 2.2
pounds (1 kg). Females are about 10% smaller and weigh up to
50% less than males.

Habitat

In this area, mink are restricted to lakes and streams in northern
New Mexico.

Life Habits

Mink are active throughout the year, mainly at night. They are
seldom seen far from water. Their dens are usually in a hole in
a river bank but may be an abandoned muskrat or beaver lodge.
They are generally solitary, and often move from place to place
in a territory that may extend a mile along a stream. Food
consists of frogs, fish, crayfish, muskrats, and other aquatic
animals. A litter (usually two to six) of blind, helpless young is
born in April or May. Their skin is in great demand in the fur
trade.

Mink

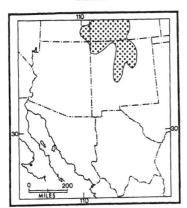

Badger

Taxidea taxus

Order Carnivora   **Family Mustelidae**

Identifying Features

This stout-bodied carnivore is well-adapted for burrowing. The legs, neck, tail, and ears are short. The forefeet have long, strong claws useful in digging. The head is broad and triangular. Color is black on the head, white on the cheeks and the wide line down the back. The back and sides are a mixture of black and white hairs.

Measurements

Total length, 31 inches (780 mm); tail, 5 inches (130 mm); hind foot, 4.3 inches (110 mm); ear, 2 inches (50 mm); weight, 20 pounds (9 kg).

Habitat

Badgers live in a variety of nonforested areas from high mountains to low deserts throughout the area.

Life Habits

Badgers are active throughout the year, mainly in late afternoon or at night. They tend to be solitary. Food consists mostly of small rodents, reptiles, and insects that are usually dug from the ground. During much of the year, badgers dig new burrows each morning for a day retreat. In the spring, females dig a deep burrow and line it with grasses. There one to five (usually two) young are born in March or April. During cold winter periods, badgers sleep for days at a time, living on fat. In captivity, they can live as long as 13 years.

Badger

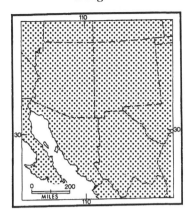

Spotted skunk

Spilogale gracilis

Order Carnivora   **Family Mustelidae**

Identifying Features

This small skunk (kitten-sized) is black with white spots, one on the forehead, one below each ear, and others variously scattered over the back and sides. The bushy tail is tipped with white.

Measurements

Total length, 17 inches (430 mm); tail, 6 inches (150 mm); hind foot, 1.8 inches (45 mm); ear, 0.8 inch (20 mm); weight, 1.2 pounds (500 g).

Habitat

Spotted skunks live below 8000 feet (2500 m) in hilly or rough, broken country. In deserts, they occur near water sources.

Life Habits

These small skunks are active at night during most of the year. In cold periods, they may stay in a den for days. Winter dens are often communal, with two or more skunks present. Food is mainly insects and other invertebrates although small lizards, rodents, fruits, and berries are eaten. A litter of two to ten (usually four) young is born in March or April. By late summer, the young accompany their mother on her nightly hunting trips. When alarmed, Spotted skunks have an unusual "handstand" reaction that results in a spectacular display of the back and tail. If the warning is unheeded, the provoker may then be sprayed from the anal scent glands.

Spotted skunk

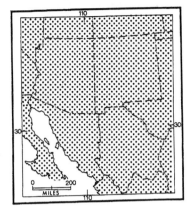

Striped skunk

Mephitis mephitis

Order Carnivora   **Family Mustelidae**

Identifying Features
This is a black, cat-sized carnivore that has white markings on the head, neck, shoulders, back, and on part of the large bushy tail. The legs are short; the movements deliberate.

Measurements
Total length, 28 inches (700 mm); tail, 11.5 inches (300 mm); hind foot, 3 inches (75 mm); ear, 1.1 inches (28 mm); weight, 6.6 pounds (3 kg). In the fall, an old, fat male may weigh up to 15 pounds (6.8 kg).

Habitat
Striped skunks live in more or less open country in woodlands, brush areas, and grasslands, usually near water.

Life Habits
These skunks are active at night throughout the year. During cold periods, they may remain in a den for days. They feed on both plant and animal material including various fruits, bird eggs, insects, worms, as well as other invertebrates. Dead animals (carrion) are a major source of food. A litter of four to ten (generally five) blind, helpless young is born in May or June. By the end of the summer, the young follow their mother on hunting trips. Dens are in holes in the ground, sometimes under a rock or a building. These skunks can live up to six years in captivity. *See related species 110.*

Striped skunk

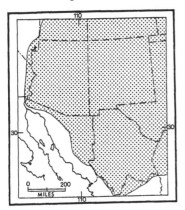

Sandy Truett

Hog-nosed skunk

Conepatus mesoleucus

Order Carnivora   **Family Mustelidae**

Identifying Features

This skunk is similar in size and general appearance to the Striped skunk. The white marking is larger, extending from the top of the head, down the back and including all of the tail. Black hairs are scattered among the white hairs of the tail. The snout is long, the nose pad is enlarged and thickened, and the top of the snout is hairless. The fur is short and coarse. The claws on the forefeet are elongated.

Measurements

Total length, 29 inches (730 mm); tail, 9 inches (230 mm); hind foot, 3 inches (75 mm); ear, 1 inch (25 mm); weight, 5 pounds (2.3 kg).

Habitat

Hog-nosed skunks live in rocky areas of the foothills and grass-lands.

Life Habits

Like other skunks, Hog-nosed skunks are active throughout the year, mostly at night. In cold weather, they stay in dens for extended periods. Dens are usually in rock crevices. Food is mainly insects that are rooted out of the ground by the thick-ened, almost piglike nose pad. Also eaten are grubs, snails, earthworms, small rodents, reptiles, and various bulbs and roots. A litter of two to four young is born in April or May.

Hog-nosed skunk

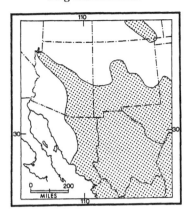

River otter

Lutra canadensis

Order Carnivora   **Family Mustelidae**

Identifying Features

This large carnivore is well-adapted for a life in and around water. The body is somewhat teardrop in shape; the ears are small. The tail is thick at the base and becomes smaller toward the tip. The toes are webbed and can be broadly spread. The hair is dense and waterproof. The back is brownish, the belly is paler.

Measurements

Total length, 51 inches (1.3 m); tail, 32 inches (820 mm); hind foot, 5.7 inches (150 mm); ear, 2 inches (50 mm); weight, 20 pounds (9 kg).

Habitat

River otters once occurred throughout this area, wherever there were permanent streams. They has been eliminated from much of their range.

Life Habits

River otters are active throughout the year, mainly at night. Almost all activity is in rivers or streams or along the adjacent bank. Their den is a hole in the bank, often under the roots of a tree from which the soil has been washed away. River otters are generally solitary. Food is mainly fish, but invertebrates, frogs, and some birds are also eaten. A litter of two to five young is born in the spring. *See related species 111.*

River otter

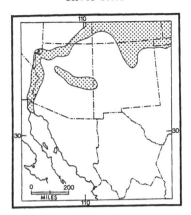

Sandy Truett

Jaguar

Felis onca

Order Carnivora   **Family Felidae**

Identifying Features

This is a large spotted cat that is about the size of the Old World Leopard. The tail is spotted, not striped. Some black (melanistic) individuals have been reported.

Measurements

Total length, 90 inches (2.3 m); tail, 26 inches (650 mm); hind foot, 11 inches (275 mm); weight, 285 pounds (130 kg). Females are 15% smaller than the males.

Habitat

Jaguars formerly occurred in the desert grasslands and lower mountains of this area but are now only rarely seen.

Life Habits

Jaguars are solitary animals that are usually active at night. As is true of most large carnivores, these cats require a large hunting range, perhaps covering 100 to 200 square miles (up to 500 square kilometers) in a year. Food consists of various large animals, especially deer and javelina, and some domestic animals may be killed. Along rivers, Jaguars scoop fish from the water. Two to four kittens are born in a litter after a gestation period of 100 days. They survive up to 22 years in captivity.

Jaguar

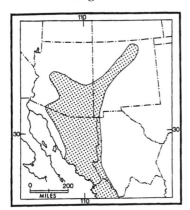

Mountain lion

Felis concolor

Order Carnivora   **Family Felidae**

Identifying Features
This is a large, unspotted, leopard-sized cat that has short yellowish-brown fur. Its long tail has a dark brown tip.

Measurements
Total length, 90 inches (2.3 m); tail, 31 inches (800 mm); hind foot, 12 inches (300 mm); ear, 4 inches (100 mm); weight, 160 pounds (70 kg). Females are about 10% smaller than the males.

Habitat
Mountain lions formerly occurred throughout most of this region. Still present in all but the most human-modified areas, they are most common in rural situations.

Life Habit
Mountain lions are active throughout the year, mostly at night. Their usual food consists of deer, rabbits, and rodents. When they are hungry, and domestic animals are available, they may kill sheep, goats, calves, pigs, cows, and even horses. A large area is needed to provide a continuing food source year after year. Feeding areas often include as much as 25 miles around the den. Populations of large cats were never high despite various old-timer tales. At present, in some areas, populations are as dense as ten animals per 100 square miles. Probably this has always been normal. Females have dens in caves or cliffs, where two to five kittens are born in the spring.

Mountain lion

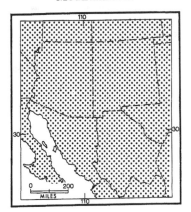

Ocelot

Felis pardalis

Order Carnivora   **Family Felidae**

Identifying Features

The Ocelot is a medium-sized long-legged cat that has a spotted coat and a ringed tail.

Measurements

Total length, 47 inches (1.2 m); tail, 14.8 inches (375 mm); hind foot, 6.7 inches (170 mm); weight, to 35 pounds (16 kg). The females are smaller than the males.

Habitat

These cats are generally restricted to densely wooded areas. They are probably now extinct in this part of their former range.

Life Habits

Like other cats, Ocelots are active throughout the year, mainly at night. They often hunt in pairs, capturing and feeding on a variety of rodents, rabbits, birds, reptiles, and frogs. Two kittens per litter is usual. *See related species 112.*

Ocelot

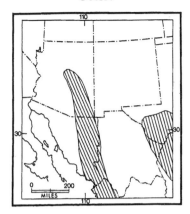

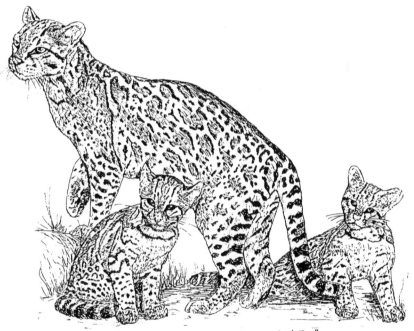

sandy Truett

Bobcat

Felis rufus

Order Carnivora   **Family Felidae**

Identifying Features

This is a short-tailed cat with tufted ears, large paws, and a large, broad head. It is larger than the house cat. The color is a reddish brown with black spots.

Measurements

Total length, 37 inches (940 mm); tail, 6 inches (150 mm); hind foot, 7.5 inches (190 mm); ear, 3 inches (80 mm); weight, 24 pounds (10.9 kg).

Habitat

Bobcats occur throughout most of this area, being most common in brush and forest-edge situations or in rocky canyons. They even occur in city suburbs.

Life Habits

Bobcats are active throughout the year, mostly at night. Food is mainly small rodents and rabbits. Squirrels, porcupines, birds, and carrion are also eaten. Rarely, lambs and small goats are killed and eaten. Most of their hunting is done within two miles of their den. Dens are in rock crevices or in holes under rocks, fallen trees, or tree stumps. Some dens are in hollow trees. After a gestation period of 50 to 60 days, a litter of one to four (usually two) blind, helpless young are born. Although most young are born in April or May, some have been born in every month of the year.

Bobcat

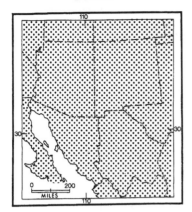

Collared peccary

Tayassu tajacu

Order Artiodactyla   **Family Tayassuidae**

Identifying Features

This piglike, hoofed mammal—also called javelina—is essentially tailless and has a well-developed mane on the shoulders and back. It has four toes on each foot, but most of the weight is borne on the central two. Males have well-developed tusks. The hair is stiff and is a grizzled grayish to blackish in color, sometimes with a yellowish wash on the hairs of the cheeks, throat, and collar.

Measurements

Total length, 36 inches (925 mm); tail, 1.5 inches (30 mm); hind foot, 7.5 (190 mm); ear, 3.5 inches (85 mm); weight, to 50 pounds (23 kg).

Habitat

Peccaries are generally found in desert grasslands and areas of dense brush, usually near a source of water.

Life Habits

Peccaries are often found in bands of three to 20, sometimes more. Food is a variety of vegetable materials including roots, bulbs, shoots, and fruits. Cactus fruit, grain, some animals, and even carrion is eaten. They "bed down" in shallow depressions in dense brush and also use shallow caves and abandoned mine tunnels as resting sites. One or two young are born in almost any month of the year. At birth, the young are reddish, with a black dorsal stripe. Peccaries can live up to 15 years in captivity.

Collared peccary

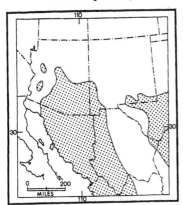

Wapiti or elk

Cervus elaphus

Order Artiodactyla   **Family Cervidae**

Identifying Features
This is a large deer that has a patch of pale yellowish hair on the rump around the small, white tail. The color is a reddish brown. Males have a mane on the neck and, in late summer and fall, large antlers. The antlers of older males generally have six branches, the lowest of which (the brow tine, nearest the head) is well-developed.

Measurements
Total length, 98 inches (2.5 m); tail, 6 inches (150 mm); hind foot, 21 inches (550 mm); ear, 8 inches (200 mm); weight, usually about 600 pounds, but over 1000 pounds (270-450 kg) has been recorded. Females are about 10% smaller than males.

Habitat
Elk live in the higher mountainous regions. Some consider that the large-antlered population of Elk exterminated in Arizona and New Mexico by 1900 was a distinct species called Merriam's elk (*Cervus merriami*). Perhaps it was only subspecifically distinct. In any case, Elk now in the region descended from animals introduced from the Yellowstone herd.

Life Habits
Elk formerly lived in herds of ten to several hundred. These herds migrated from high mountain meadows in the summer to lowlands in the winter. Food is a variety of grasses, sedges, and fresh growth on bushes and trees. A single calf, born in May or June, weighs about 30 pounds (13.5 kg) and is brownish with light spots.

Wapiti or elk

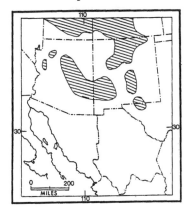

sandy Truett

Mule deer

Odocoileus hemionus

Order Artiodactyla   **Family Cervidae**

Identifying Features

This deer is smaller than the Elk. Its tail is narrow and mostly white, but with at least a black tip, if not black on the whole top surface. Color is a reddish brown in the summer, grayish in the winter. Males have antlers from late summer until January. The main forks of the antlers are equally branched.

Measurements

Total length, 63 inches (1.6 m); tail, 8 inches (200 mm); hind foot, 18 inches (450 mm); ear, 8 inches (200 mm); weight, to 350 pounds (150 kg).

Habitat

Mule deer occur from coniferous forests down to shrubby grass-lands and desert areas. They are found most often in broken country, generally in brush or at a forest edge.

Life Habits

Mule deer are active mainly in the early morning and late evening, or on moonlit nights. They move to higher mountain elevations during the spring and summer. In the fall and winter, they often live in small herds. They feed mostly on shrubs and twigs, but also eat some grasses and herbs. After a gestation period of about 210 days, one or two young are born. At birth, the fawns are furred, have their eyes open, and can follow their mother within minutes.

Mule deer

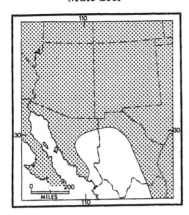

Sandy Truett

White-tailed deer

Odocoileus virginianus

Order Artiodactyla   **Family Cervidae**

Identifying Features

This deer has shorter ears and a longer tail than the Mule deer. The tail is brownish above, white below, and has a white tip. When running, the white tail, held erect, is extremely evident. The belly, throat, inside of the ears, and the rings around the eyes and nose are white. The antlers on the males have a main beam with smaller branches (tines) growing out from it.

Measurements

Total length, 67 inches (1.7 m); tail, 10 inches (250 mm); hind foot, 16 inches (410 mm); ear, 2 inches (50 mm); weight, 120 pounds (55 kg).

Habitat

In this region, White-tailed deer are most common in grasslands, meadows, oak woodlands, and broken terrain.

Life Habits

White-tailed deer are similar in habits to the Mule deer. They are usually active in the morning and evening and on moonlit nights. Most of their life is spent in a small home area of about one square mile. Food consists of green plants, acorns, as well as brush and twigs. One to three young are born after a gestation period of about 200 days. Captive animals live as long as 20 years.

White-tailed deer

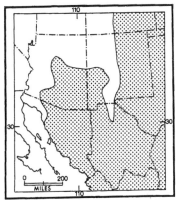

Sandy Truett

Pronghorn

Antilocapra americana

Order Artiodactyla   **Family Bovidae**

Identifying Features

The Pronghorn is a hoofed mammal that is slightly smaller than the Mule deer. It has black horns—not antlers—both in females and males. Unlike the horns of the Bison and sheep, the outer portion (horn sheath) is shed each year. The color is brownish. A large, white rump patch, and two bands across the throat are characteristic.

Measurements

Total length, 53 inches (1.3 m); tail, 6 inches (150 mm); hind foot, 17 inches (425 mm); weight, to 125 pounds (57 kg).

Habitat

Pronghorns are residents of bushy grasslands and sagebrush flats.

Life Habits

Pronghorns are active during most parts of the day. They feed on a wide variety of brush and forbs as well as some grasses. Sagebrush and rabbit brush are favorites. In much of their range, they move down slopes to valleys to spend the winter months. They move in herds, with groups of ten to 60 being common. For short distances, Pronghorns can run 55 miles per hour (88 kph). After a gestation period of about eight months, one or two young are born, usually in June. They can follow their mother within minutes of birth. In captivity, Pronghorns can live up to 15 years.

Pronghorn

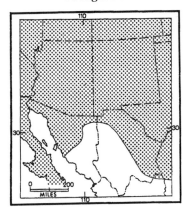

Sandy Truett

Bison

Bison bison

Order Artiodactyla   **Family Bovidae**

Identifying Features

The Bison, also called American buffalo, is almost cowlike in appearance but is generally larger and chunkier. Its horns (in both males and females) are bent outward and upward. The forehead and neck are short, the face broad. The shoulders have a large hump. Hair on the shoulders, head, and neck is long and the chin is bearded. The tail is short and tufted. The color is dark brownish.

Measurements

Total length, 11 feet (3.4 m); tail, 25 inches (625 mm); hind foot, 24 inches (600 mm); weight, to 1800 pounds (820 kg). Females are generally about one-third smaller than the males.

Habitat

Bison once occurred in the grasslands of eastern New Mexico southward into eastern Chihuahua. They were probably eliminated from the region more than a century ago. Today, small, isolated herds are sometimes kept on ranches.

Life Habits

In the past, Bison occurred in herds that seasonally moved north and south in the Great Plains to take advantage of available food. In parts of the range, this led to temporary local concentrations that caused some hunters and writers to think that Bison populations were limitless. Some recent guesses place the original population at about 60 million. By 1890, the total was less than 1000.

Bison

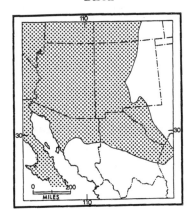

Mountain sheep

Ovis canadensis

Order Artiodactyla   **Family Bovidae**

Identifying Features

The Mountain sheep is a large sheep that has large, heavy-curving horns in males (more slender and less curved in females). It is brownish to grayish in color and has a large white rump patch.

Measurements

Total length, 70 inches (1.8 m); tail, 5 inches (130 mm); hind foot, 16 inches (420 mm); weight, to 300 pounds (140 kg). Females are 15% smaller than the males.

Habitat

Mountain sheep, also called Bighorn sheep, once lived in most of the foothills and mountains. In competition with man and domestic animals, they have been eliminated from much of the area.

Life Habits

Most feeding by Mountain sheep occurs in the early morning, but they may be active any time of the day. Food is a mixture of grasses, branches of woody plants, and various herbs. They generally occur in small bands. Some large bands include 12 to 15, or even more, individuals. Their need for drinking water restricts their occurrence in desert regions. After a gestation period of about six months, a single lamb is born in March or April.

Mountain sheep

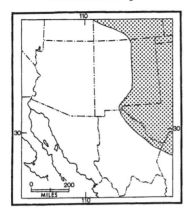

Sandy Truett

Related Species

The following mammals could all have been listed in the preceding pages. However, most are not only close relatives to the ones discussed above, but also much like their "relative" in size and appearance. In some cases, the "major species" listed above does not occur throughout the region, but is often replaced by one of these "related species." Obviously, in such places, the "related species" should be given a "major" status.

1. **Grayish mouse opossum** (*Marmosa canesens*). This is a tiny opossum with soft grey fur and no long, coarse, white hairs. Measurements: total length, 11 inches (275 mm); tail, 6 inches (150 mm); hind foot, 0.9 inch (20 mm). Map 1b.

2. **Northern water shrew** (*Sorex palustris*). This is a large shrew: length, 6 inches (150 mm); tail, 3 inches (75 mm); hind foot, 0.75 inch (20 mm); weight, 0.5 ounce (15 g). It lives in and near mountain streams. The body is black to gray above, lighter below. The tail is bicolored, dark above. The hind feet have a fringe of stiff hairs that help trap air bubbles, permitting this shrew to walk on the surface of water for short distances. Map 1a.

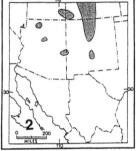

3. **Dwarf shrew** (*Sorex nanus*). This small shrew weighs only about 0.1 ounce (3 g). It occurs mainly at elevations of 7000 to 9000 feet (2100-2700 m) where it is generally associated with bogs and marshes. Map 2.

4. **Merriam's shrew** (*Sorex merriami*). This shrew is smaller than the Vagrant shrew. It usually lives in drier places than most other shrews—open sagebrush, grasslands, dry woodlands. It is light-colored, gray above and white below. The tail is white. Measurements: total length, 3.8 inches (95 mm); tail, 1.5 inches (37 mm); hind foot, 0.5 inch (12 mm); weight, 0.2 ounce (5 g). Map 3a.

5. **Arizona shrew** (*Sorex arizonae*). Similar to Merriam's shrew. Map 3b.

6. **Masked shrew** (*Sorex cinereus*). This species is about the size of the Vagrant shrew. It differs in the size of some small teeth in the anterior part of the jaw, in being lighter in color (brown-

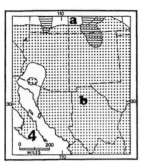

ish to grayish tan), and other more obscure features. It occurs in the high mountains of northern New Mexico. Map 4a.

7. **Desert shrew** (*Notiosorex crawfordi*). This is a small shrew that has larger ears than other shrews. It occurs in semiarid situations. Measurements: total length, 3.5 inches (90 mm); tail, 1.4 inches (35 mm); hind foot, 0.5 inch (12 mm); weight, 0.2 ounce (4.5 g). Map 4b.

8. **Parnell's mustached bat** (*Pteronotus parnellii*). These bats have an unmodified chin. Measurements: total length, 3.1 inches (63 mm); tail, 0.8 inch (19 mm); hind foot, 0.5 inch (13 mm); ear, 1 inch (25 mm); forearm, 2.2 inches (55 mm); weight, 0.5 ounce (15 g). The ears are connected by two low, inconspicuous ridges. The wings are attached to the side of the body; the tail is only about half the length of the interfemoral membrane. The chin, tail, ears, and forearm are similar to those of the Naked-backed bat. Not mapped—distribution similar to map 5a.

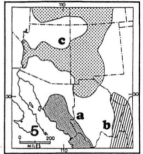

9. **Wagner's mustached bat** (*Pteronotus personatus*). Size similar to Parnell's mustached bat. Measurements: total length, 3.1 inches (79 mm); tail, 0.8 inch (19 mm); hind foot, 0.5 inch (13 mm); ear, 1 inch (23 mm); forearm, 2.2 inches (55 mm); weight, 0.5 ounce (15 g). Wing membrane are attached high on the sides, resulting in a narrow strip of fur visible on the back. Ears connected as in Parnell's bat. Not mapped—distribution similar to map 1b.

10. **Naked-backed bat** (*Pteronotus davyi*). The wings are attached to the midline of the back, just above the backbone. The result is a naked appearance of the back and sides when viewed from above. The tip of the tail is free on the top surface of the interfemoral membrane. The ears are small, not noticeably connected at the bases. Measurements: total length, 2.9 inches (74 mm); tail, inch 0.8 (20 mm); hind foot, 0.4 inch (11 mm); ear, 0.7 inch (17 mm); forearm, 1.8 inches (45 mm); weight, 0.3 ounce (9 g). Map 5a.

11. **Peter's bat** (*Balantiopteryx plicata*). In the family Emballonuridae, this is a plain-nosed bat with a primitive wing structure and attachment. The snout region is greatly inflated and a white edge is on the wing membrane. Measurements: total length, 2.5 inches (63 mm); tail, 0.6 inch (14 mm); hind foot, 0.2 inch (6 mm); ear, 0.5 inch (13 mm); forearm, 1.5 inches (40 mm); weight, 0.3 ounce (7.5 g). Not mapped—distribution similar to map 1b.

176

12. **Yellow-shouldered bat** (*Sturnira lilium*). This is a leaf-nosed bat, family Phyllostomidae. Measurements: total length, 2.6 inches (65 mm); tail, absent; hind foot, 0.6 inch (14 mm); ear, 0.7 inch (17 mm); forearm, 1.6 inches (41 mm); weight, 0.7 ounce (20 g). Not mapped—distribution similar to map 1b.

13. **Salvin's white-lined bat** (*Chiroderma salvini*). A leaf-nosed bat, family Phyllostomidae, with a dark brown back that has a white stripe from the nape of the neck to the base of the tail. Measurements: total length, 2.6 inches (66 mm); tail, absent; hind foot, 0.5 inch (13 mm); ear, 0.7 inch (17 mm); forearm, 1.8 inches (45 mm); weight, 0.7 ounce (21 g). In this area, only known from southernmost Chihuahua. No map.

14. **Hairy fruit-eating bat** (*Artibeus hirsutus*). Leaf-nosed bat, family Phyllostomidae. Measurements: total length, 2.9 inches (73 mm); tail, absent; hind foot, 0.6 inch (15 mm); ear, 0.8 inch (20 mm); forearm, 2.1 inches (53 mm); weight, 1 ounce (29 g). Not mapped—distribution similar to map 5a.

15. **Vampire bat** (*Desmodus rotundus*). Leaf-nosed bat, family Phyllostomidae (some authorities) or separate family Desmodontidae. This bat feeds on blood of warm-blooded vertebrates. Measurements: total length, 3 inches (77 mm); tail, absent; hind foot, 0.7 inch (18 mm); ear, 0.7 inch (18 mm); forearm, 2.2 inches (58 mm); weight, 1.1 ounces (30 g). Not mapped—distribution similar to map 1b.

16. **Mexican funnel-eared bat** (*Natalus stramineus*). This is a plain-nosed bat in the family Natalidae. Its ears are large and funnel shaped. Measurements: total length, 3.9 inches (98 mm); tail, 2 inches (51 mm); hind foot, 0.4 inch (9 mm); ear, 0.6 inch (14 mm); forearm, 1.5 inches (37 mm); weight, 0.2 ounce (6 g). Not mapped—distribution similar to map 5a.

17. **Waterhouse's leaf-nosed bat** (*Macrotus waterhousii*). This native of the southernmost part of the region differs from the California leaf-nosed bat in minor details including structure of its chromosomes. Not mapped—distribution similar to map 5a.

18. **Shrew-faced bat** (*Glossophaga soricina*). These leaf-nosed bats are smaller and have a shorter rostrum than the Long-tongued bat. Measurements: total length, 2.5 inches (63 mm); tail, 0.4 inch (10 mm); hind foot, 0.4 inch (11 mm); ear, 0.6 inch (16 mm); forearm, 1.5 inches (37 mm); weight, 0.4 ounce (10 g). The tail extends only about half the length of the interfemoral membrane. Food consists primarily of insects with some ripe fruit being eaten. Not mapped—distribution similar to map 1b.

19. **Mexican long-nosed bat** (*Leptonycteris nivalis*). This species is quite similar to the Lesser long-nosed bat. It is only slightly larger and has slightly longer wings. Map 5b.

20. **Little brown bat** (*Myotis lucifugus*). Slightly larger than the California myotis. Map 5c.

21. Western small-footed myotis (*Myotis ciliolabrum*). This bat has a shorter forearm (about 1.5 inches–37 mm) and weighs less (0.2 ounce–6 g) than the Little brown bat. Day roosts are often in tiny rock crevices, usually in forested areas. Map 6.

22. Yuma myotis (*Myotis yumanensis*). This bat is about the same size as the Little brown bat. It feeds almost exclu-

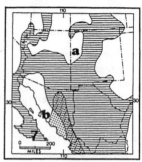

sively on insects that are captured as they fly over permanent streams and ponds. Map 7a.

23. Cinnamon myotis (*Myotis fortidens*). Size much like the Little brown bat. Map 7b.

24. Cave myotis (*Myotis velifer*). A larger bat than the Little brown bat, its summer roosts are in mines and caves. Measurements: total length, 3.8 inches (95 mm); tail, 1.6 inches (42 mm); hind foot, 0.4 inch (10 mm); ear, 0.6 inch (14

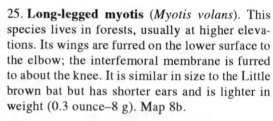

mm); forearm, 1.6 inches (42 mm); weight, 0.4 ounce (12 g). Map 8a.

25. Long-legged myotis (*Myotis volans*). This species lives in forests, usually at higher elevations. Its wings are furred on the lower surface to the elbow; the interfemoral membrane is furred to about the knee. It is similar in size to the Little brown bat but has shorter ears and is lighter in weight (0.3 ounce–8 g). Map 8b.

26. Fringed myotis (*Myotis thysanodes*). This bat has longer ears (0.7 inch–18 mm) and forearms (1.7 inches–44 mm) than the Little brown bat. It has a well-developed fringe of stiff hairs extending from the edge of the interfemoral membrane. Map 9.

27. Long-eared myotis (*Myotis evotis*). This bat has longer ears (0.9 inch–23 mm), longer forearms (1.6 inches–40 mm), and lighter weight (0.25 ounce–7 g) than the Little brown bat. Its ears, black in color, are longer than any Myotis in the area. Coniferous forests are its usual habitat. Map 10a.

28. Southwestern myotis (*Myotis auriculus*). Map 10b.

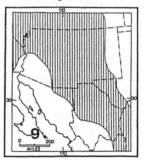

178

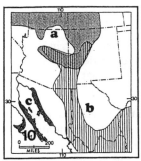

29. **Fish-eating bat** (*Myotis vivesi*). A large myotis that feeds on crustaceans and small fish from the Gulf of California that are captured by the elongated claws of the hind feet. Measurements: total length, 5.5 inches (140 mm). Map 10c.

30. **Little yellow bat** (*Rhogeessa parvula*). Measurements: total length, 2.8 inches (70 mm); tail, 1.2 inches (30 mm); hind foot, 0.2 inch (6 mm); ear, 0.5 inch (12 mm); forearm, 1.1 inches (27 mm); weight, 0.1 ounce (3 g). Not mapped—distribution similar to map 1b.

31. **Allen's big-eared bat** (*Idionycteris phyllotis*). This rarely seen bat is larger and has longer ears than Townsend's big-eared bat. It weighs about 0.45 ounce (13 g) and has ears that are about 1.5 inches (40 mm) in length. Map 11a.

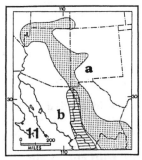

32. **Mexican big-eared bat** (*Plecotus mexicanus*). This species is slightly smaller than Townsend's lump-nosed bat. Map 11b.

33. **Peale's free-tailed bat** (*Tadarida aurispinosa*). Similar in size to the Brazilian free-tailed bat. Not mapped—distribution similar to map 1b.

34. **Big free-tailed bat** (*Nyctinomops macrotis*). This species is even larger than the Pocketed free-tailed bat, with a forearm that is 1.4 inches (60 mm) in length and a weight of 0.9 ounce (25 g). Its ears are broadly joined at the midline. Day roosts are generally in high rock crevices. Throughout area, not mapped.

35. **Pocketed free-tailed bat** (*Nyctinomops femorosaccus*). This species is larger than the Brazilian free-tailed bat. Its ears are joined at their bases. Measurements: total length, 4 inches (100 mm); tail, 1.5 inches (38 mm);

hind foot, 0.4 inch (9 mm); forearm, 1.9 inches (47 mm); weight, 0.5 ounce (16 g). Map 12a.

36. **Underwood's mastiff bat** (*Eumops underwoodi*). Size slightly smaller than Greater mastiff bat. Measurements: total length, 6.3 inches (160 mm); hind foot, 1.4 inches (35 mm); forearm, 2.6 inches (70 mm); weight, 2.1 ounces (60 g). Map 12b.

179

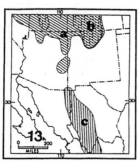

37. **Desert cottontail** (*Sylvilagus audubonii*). This cottontail is slightly smaller (weight, 2 pounds–900 g) and lighter in color than Nuttall's cottontail. It usually lives in desert grasslands. Not mapped, occurs throughout area at elevations below 4000 feet (1300 m).

38. **Nuttall's cottontail** (*Sylvilagus nuttallii*). This cottontail is similar to the Eastern cottontail but with the inner surface of the ear densely furred. It is usually found at elevations above 6000 feet (1800 m) in treeless, brush-covered areas. Map 13a.

39. **Snowshoe hare** (*Lepus americanus*). This hare has relatively small ears and is darker- colored than the other hares (jack rabbits). The ears are black-tipped. Map 13b.

40. **White-tailed jack rabbit** (*Lepus townsendii*). This jack rabbit is usually found at higher elevations (above 6000 feet–1800 m) than the black-tailed jack rabbit. The top of the tail is white. Map 13c.

41. **White-sided jack rabbit** (*Lepus callotis*). This species is slightly smaller than the Antelope jack rabbit. Its distribution is in the Chihuahuan Desert, east of the Sierra Madre Mountains. Not mapped.

42. **Cliff chipmunk** (*Tamias dorsalis*). This is a grayish chipmunk with indistinct stripes on its body. It is often seen at lower elevations of the mountains and is more restricted to rocky areas than most other chipmunks. Map 14a.

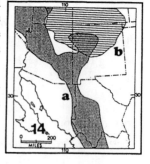

43. **Colorado chipmunk** (*Tamias quadrivittatus*). This chipmunk is much like the Uinta chipmunk in appearance and habits. Map 14b.

44. **Gray-footed chipmunk** (*Tamias canipes*). Map 15a.

45. **Gray-collared chipmunk** (*Tamias cinereicollis*). Map 15b.

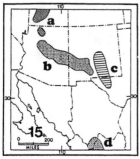

46. **Uinta chipmunk** (*Tamias umbrinus*). This chipmunk differs only in minor details from several other species. Map 15c.

47. **Buller's chipmunk** (*Tamias bulleri*). Much like the Gray-collared chipmunk. In this area, occurs only in the southeasternmost part of Chihuahua. Map 15d.

180

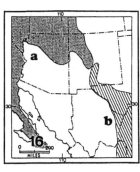

48. **White-tailed antelope squirrel** (*Ammospermophilus leucurus*). Similar to the Texas antelope squirrel. Map 16a.

49. **Texas antelope squirrel** (*Ammospermophilus interpres*). Much like the Harris antelope squirrel, but with a white area on the middle of the underside of the tail. Map 16b.

50. **Spotted ground squirrel** (*Spermophilus spilosoma*). Like the Thirteen-lined ground squirrel in size and shape, this species is light brown in color with indistinct roundish white spots on the back and rump. Map 17a.

51. **Mexican ground squirrel** (*Spermophilus mexicanus*). Map 17b.

52. **Sierra Madre ground squirrel** (*Spermophilus madrensis*). Map 17c.

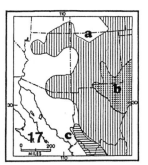

53. **Black-tailed prairie dog** (*Cynomys ludovicianus*). This prairie dog is primarily an inhabitant of the Great Plains of the United States. Unlike other species that occur in this area, it has a distinct, black-tipped tail. Populations are reduced to scattered colonies. Map 18.

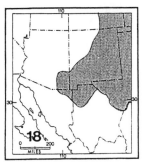

54. **Fox squirrel** (*Sciurus niger*). This species, a native of the eastern United States, has been introduced into various city parks. The large bushy tail with buff-tipped hairs is distinctive. It is the largest North American tree squirrel. Measurements: total length, 23.6 inches (600 mm); tail, 10.8 inches (275 mm); hind foot, 3 inches (75 mm); weight, 1.8 pounds (800 g). No map.

55. **Eastern gray squirrel** (*Sciurus carolinensis*). This native of the eastern United States has been successfully introduced into a few parks in this region. Measurements: total length, 19 inches (480 mm); tail, 9 inches (225 mm); hind foot, 2.6 inches (65 mm); weight, 2 pounds (900 g). The tail bush appears to be flattened and has long gray hairs that are tipped with white, giving a silvery appearance. No map.

56. **Northern pocket gopher** (*Thomomys talpoides*). In general, a given area has only a single kind of pocket gopher. Even when two species do occur in the same general region, they occupy different habitats. This

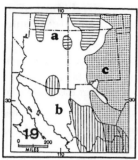

species inhabits mountain meadows and other high elevation sites when they occur near another species of pocket gopher. Map 19a.

57. Southern pocket gopher (*Thomomys umbrinus*). Very much like Botta's pocket gopher. Map 19b.

58. Yellow-faced pocket gopher (*Pappogeomys castanops*). Like other pocket gophers, this species is rarely seen aboveground. Its upper incisors have only a single vertical groove on the front surface. Map 19c.

59. Plains pocket gopher (*Geomys bursarius*). This species is an inhabitant of the Great Plains. It is restricted to the lower elevations of the eastern part of this region. Its upper incisors have two obvious vertical grooves on the front surface. Map 20a.

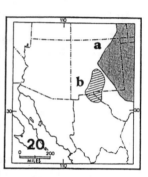

60. Desert pocket gopher (*Geomys arenarius*). Similar to the Plains pocket gopher. Map 20b.

61. Great Basin pocket mouse (*Perognathus parvus*). Measurements of this silky pocket

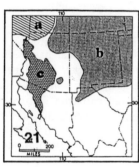

mouse are: total length, 6.9 inches (175 mm); tail, 3.3 inches (85 mm); hind foot, 1 inch (25 mm); weight, 0.8 ounce (22 g). Map 21a.

62. Plains pocket mouse (*Perognathus flavescens*). This small pocket mouse has soft fur. Measurements: total length, 5.1 inches (130 mm); tail, 2.1 inches (55 mm); hind foot, 0.6 inch (18 mm); ear, 0.2 inch (6 mm); weight, 0.3 ounce (8 g). Map 21b.

63. Arizona pocket mouse (*Perognathus amplus*). Map 21c.

64. Little pocket mouse (*Perognathus longimembris*). In this area, this small species occurs only in southwestern Arizona and northwestern Sonora. Map 22a.

65. Long-tailed pocket mouse (*Perognathus formosus*). The pelage of this large species is harsher than that of most *Perognathus*. Measurements: total length, 8 inches (200 mm); tail, 4 inches (100 mm); hind foot, 1 inch (25 mm); weight, 0.8 ounce (21 g). Map 22b.

66. **Bailey's pocket mouse** (*Chaetodipus baileyi*). This is the largest pocket mouse in the area. Measurements: total length, 7.9 inches (200 mm); tail, 4.1 inches (110 mm); hind foot, 1 inch (25 mm); ear, 0.4 inch (9 mm); weight, 1 ounce (28 g). Map 23a.

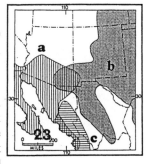

67. **Hispid pocket mouse** (*Chaetodipus hispidus*). This large spiny-haired pocket mouse is a dark buff brown. The tail is slightly shorter than the head and body and it has a poorly developed tuft of hairs at the tip. It lives in grasslands and desert grasslands. Measurements: total length, 8.2 inches (210 mm); tail, 4 inches (100 mm); weight, 1.2 ounces (36 g). Map 23b.

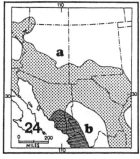

68. **Goldman's pocket mouse** (*Chaetodipus goldmani*). Size larger than the Rock pocket mouse. Map 23c.

69. **Desert pocket mouse** (*Chaetodipus penicillatus*). This spiny pocket mouse occurs in more sandy conditions, especially along dry streambeds or washes in the deserts. Measurements: total length, 6 inches (150 mm); weight, 0.7 ounce (19 g). Map 24a.

70. **Sinaloan pocket mouse** (*Chaetodipus pernix*). Resembles the Desert pocket mouse in size. Map 24b.

71. **Nelson's pocket mouse** (*Chaetodipus nelsoni*). Slightly larger than the Rock pocket mouse. Map 25b.

72. **Narrow-skulled pocket mouse** (*Chaetodipus artus*). Similar to, but slightly smaller than, Goldman's pocket mouse. Map 25c.

73. **Painted spiny pocket mouse** (*Liomys pictus*). Not mapped, distribution similar to Goldman's pocket mouse. Map 23c.

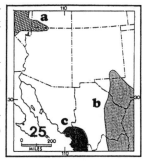

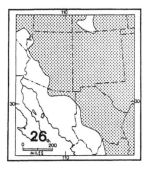

74. **Ord's kangaroo rat** (*Dipodomys ordii*). This species occurs mostly in open grasslands. Measurements: total length, 9.5 inches (240 mm) tail, 5.5 inches (140 mm); hind foot, 1.5 inches (37 mm); ear, 0.5 inch (14 mm); weight, 1.5 ounces (42 g). Map 26.

75. **Chisel-toothed kangaroo rat** (*Dipodomys microps*). This species occurs in sagebrush and Piñon-juniper woodlands. It is larger than Ord's

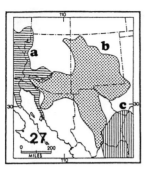

kangaroo rat. Measurements: total length, 11 inches (280 mm); tail, 6.7 inches (170 mm); hind foot, 1.7 inches (42 mm); weight, 2.2 ounces (60 g). Map 25a.

76. Desert kangaroo rat (*Dipodomys deserti*). This is a large species that lives in areas of loose sandy desert soil. Measurements: length, 13 inches (325 mm); weight, 4.2 ounces (120 g). Map 27a.

77. Banner-tailed kangaroo rat (*Dipodomys spectabilis*). This large kangaroo rat has a distinctive large, white-tipped tail. Measurements: total length, 13 inches (325 mm); tail, 8 inches (200 mm); hind foot, 2 inches (50 mm); weight, 4 ounces (110 g). Map 27b.

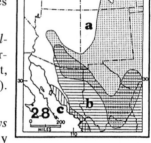

78. Nelson's kangaroo rat (*Dipodomys nelsoni*). This species is smaller than the Banner-tailed kangaroo rat. Measurements: hind foot, 1.9 inches (48 mm); weight, 3.9 ounces (110 g). Map 27c.

79. Plains harvest mouse (*Reithrodontomys montanus*). This harvest mouse differs only slightly from the Western harvest mouse. It lives in more open areas of short, dense grasses, is lighter in color, and has a very narrow dorsal tail stripe. Map 28a.

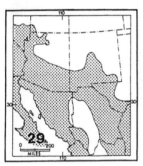

80. Burt's harvest mouse (*Reithrodontomys burti*). Similar to the Plains harvest mouse. Map 28c.

81. Fulvous harvest mouse (*Reithrodontomys fulvescens*). Larger and more brightly colored than the Western harvest mouse. Map 28b.

82. Cactus mouse (*Peromyscus eremicus*). This species occurs in the sandy soils of low deserts. Measurements: total length, 7.5 inches (190 mm); tail, 3.9 inches (100 mm); hind foot, 0.8 inch (20 mm); ear, 0.8 inch (19 mm); weight, 0.7 ounce (21 g). Map 29.

83. Canyon mouse (*Peromyscus crinitus*). This species differs from the Deer mouse in having longer, softer fur and a tufted tail that is more than half of the total length. It occurs on rocky slopes and canyon walls in situations not normally occupied by other mice of the genus *Peromyscus*. Map 30a.

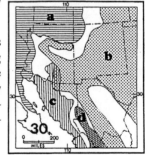

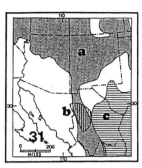

84. **White-footed mouse** (*Peromyscus leucopus*). This species is most common in the woodlands of the eastern United States. In this region, it occurs along washes and streams in the lower woodland zone. Its tail is shorter than the head and body, has no tuft, and has a wide dark strip on the top. Map 30b.

85. **Merriam's mouse** (*Peromyscus merriami*). This mouse is usually associated with dense stands of mesquites. Map 30c.

86. **Black-eared mouse** (*Peromyscus melanotus*). This is a mountaintop dweller that resembles the Deer mouse. Map 30d.

87. **Piñon mouse** (*Peromyscus truei*). This long-eared mouse occurs in rocky areas of Piñon-juniper in most nondesert habitats of this region. Measurements: total length, 8.3 inches (210 mm); tail, 4 inches (100 mm); hind foot, 1 inch (25 mm); ear, 1 inch (25 mm); weight, 1 ounce (28 g). Map 31a.

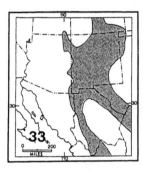

88. **Chihuahuan mouse** (*Peromyscus polius*). Map 31b.

89. **White-ankled mouse** (*Peromyscus pectoralis*). Map 31c.

90. **Brush mouse** (*Peromyscus boylii*). This species lives in rocky areas in brush and forests. Its tail is tufted and is slightly longer than the head and body. Measurements: total length, 7.8 inches (190 mm); tail, 4 inches (100 mm); hind foot, 0.8 inch (20 mm); ear, 0.8 inch (20 mm); weight, 0.9 ounce (29 g). Map 32.

91. **Rock mouse** (*Peromyscus difficilus*). Map 33.

92. **Northern grasshopper mouse** (*Onychomys leucogaster*). This species is slightly larger and shorter-tailed than the Southern grasshopper mouse. Map 34a.

93. **Mearn's grasshopper mouse** (*Onychomys arenicola*). Map 34b.

94. **Arizona cotton rat** (*Sigmodon arizonae*). Externally, it differs from the Hispid cotton rat in a few minor nonobvious features. In the structure

185

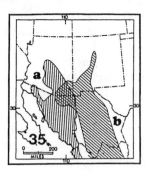

of its chromosomes, the differences are markedly distinct. Map 35a.

95. Tawny-bellied cotton rat (*Sigmodon fuliventer*). Map 35b.

96. Yellow-nosed cotton rat (*Sigmodon ochrognathus*). Map 36a.

97. Rice rat (*Oryzomys palustrus*). This small rat lives in marshlands. It is semiaquatic and has a long scaly tail that is lighter on the bottom than on the top. Measurements: total length, 11.8 inches (300 mm); tail, 5.9 inches (150 mm); hind foot, 1.4 inches (35 mm). Map 36b.

98. Desert woodrat (*Neotoma lepida*). This rat-tailed woodrat lives in desert and piñon-junipers. Map 37a.

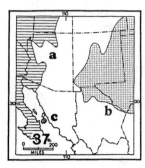

99. Southern plains woodrat (*Neotoma micropus*). Map 37b.

100. Turner Island woodrat (*Neotoma varia*). Map 37c.

101. Stephen's woodrat (*Neotoma stephensi*). Map 38.

102. Mexican woodrat (*Neotoma mexicana*). Map 39a.

103. Sonoran woodrat (*Neotoma phenax*). Map 39b.

104. Montane vole (*Microtus montanus*). This short-tailed (1.7 inches–42 mm) vole lives in burrows around the bases of grasses, especially in mountain meadows from 4000 to over 10,000 feet (1300-3300 m). Map 40.

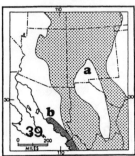

105. Meadow vole (*Microtus pennsylvanicus*). This short-tailed (1.9 inches–45 mm) relative of the Long-tailed vole occurs in much the same area. Where the two occur together, this species is found in moist habitats—marshes, bogs, and swamps. Map 41a.

186

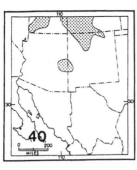

106. Prairie vole (*Microtus ochrogaster*). This short-tailed (1.4 inches–35 mm) vole is an inhabitant of the lower grasslands in the eastern portion of this region. Map 41b.

107. Mexican vole (*Microtus mexicanus*). In this region, this short-tailed (1.2 inches–30 mm) vole occurs in mountainous areas. Map 41c.

108. Black rat (*Rattus rattus*). This is also an introduced species from the Old World. It has a longer tail and longer ears than the Norway rat. It is found most commonly in large cities, especially around seaports. No map.

109. Swift fox (*Vulpes velox*). The Kit and Swift fox are so closely related that some biologists consider them to be in a single species. Map 42a.

110. Hooded skunk (*Mephitis macroura*). This species is slightly smaller but similar in appearance to the Striped skunk. It generally occurs in more rocky habitats. Map 42b.

111. Southern river otter (*Lutra annectens*). Map 43.

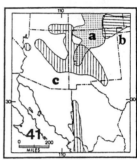

112. Margay (*Felis wiedii*). This is a small spotted cat. Measurements: total length 38 inches (1.1 m); tail, 17 inches (450 mm). Females are smaller. Not mapped—similar to map 1b.

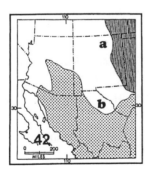

187

Suggested Readings

A Field Guide to Animal Tracks, by O. J. Murie. 1974. Houghton Mifflin Co. second edition, pp. xxi + 375.

A Field Guide to the Mammals, by William H. Burt and R. P. Grossenheider. 1976 (third edition). Houghton Mifflin. pp. xxvii + 289.

Book of Mammals. 1981. National Geographic Society, vol. one, A-J. vol. two, K-Z.

Checklist of the Vertebrates of the United States, The U. S. Territories, and Canada by R. C. Banks, R. W. McDiamid and A. L. Gardner. 1987. U.S. Department of Interior Fish and Wildlife Service Resource Publication 166. 79 pages.

Guide to Mammals, edited by Sydney Anderson. 1983. Simon and Schuster, pages 1-512.

Mammals of Arizona, by D. F. Hoffmeister. 1986. University of Arizona Press, Tucson, pp. xx+ 602.

Mammals of Chihuahua, taxonomy and distribution, by S. Anderson. 1972. Bulletin of the American Museum of Natural History, volume 7, pp. 149-410.

Mammals of Nevada, by E. R. Hall, 1946. University of California Press, pp. xi + 710.

Mammals of New Mexico, by J. S. Findley, A. H. Harris, D. E. Wilson and C. Jones. 1975. University of New Mexico Press, Albuquerque, pp xxii + 360.

Mammals of the Southwest, by E. L. Cockrum, 1982. University of Arizona Press, Tucson. pp. 1-176.

The Audubon Society Field Guide to North American Mammals, by J. D. Whitaker, Jr. 1980. Alfred A. Knopf, pp. 1-745.

The Mammals of North America, by E. R. Hall, 1981. John Wiley & Sons, 2 volumes, pp. 1-1181 plus others.

Wild Animals of North America. 1979. National Geographic Society, pages 1-406.

Index

Names in **bold face** type are the major species of this book. Names in *italics* are those listed in the related species section. All are the "common names" that occur in the publication cited in the earlier pages. The names that are given in normal type have been used in other publications, or are in common usage, that may refer to the mammal indicated.

Unfortunately, common (or vernacular) names are not always readily associated with a given species, plant, or animal. In some cases, a single species is known by as many as 30 different "common" names, often depending upon where the species occurs. Further, a single common name may be used for widely differing species, especially in different parts of the world. For example, most zoologists restrict the common name antelope to various Old World near-relatives of our bison and bighorn sheep. The North American antelope is not a near-relative and is generally referred to as a pronghorn.